The Joy of Lesbian Sex

A FIRESIDE BOOK
PUBLISHED BY SIMON AND SCHUSTER

The Joy of Lesbian Sex

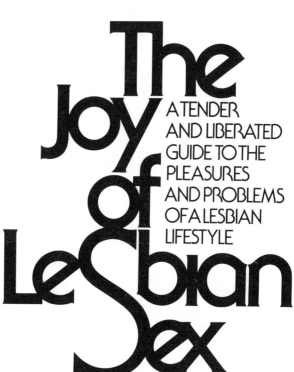

A TENDER
AND LIBERATED
GUIDE TO THE
PLEASURES
AND PROBLEMS
OF A LESBIAN
LIFESTYLE

DR. EMILY L. SISLEY
& BERTHA HARRIS

Illustrated by Yvonne Gilbert,
Charles Raymond & Patricia Faulkner

Manufactured in the United States of America

6 7 8 9 10

Library of Congress Cataloging in Publication Data

Sisley, Emily L.
  The joy of lesbian sex.

  (A Fireside book)
  Bibliography: p.
  Includes index.
  1. Lesbianism.   I. Harris, Bertha, 1937 – joint
author.   II. Title.
HQ75.5.S57   1978   301.41'57   78-6088
ISBN 0-671-24080-3

The illustrations on pp. 17-32 are by Yvonne Gilbert; those
on pp. 49-52, 85-8, 137-40 and 173-6 by Patricia Faulkner;
the line drawings throughout are by Charles Raymond.

Acknowledgements Although this book is called *The Joy of Lesbian Sex*, we do not seek to imply that the authors and editor of *The Joy of Sex* share a lesbian view of sexual satisfaction, nor that they give their blessing to this book.

Years of reading, study, dialogue, conversation and personal experience formed the two consciousnesses that finally conceived and wrote this book. We are particularly grateful, however, to those who have pioneered in revealing the true nature of woman's sexuality: Simone de Beauvoir, Betty Dodson, Shere Hite, Virginia Johnson, Alfred Kinsey, Ann Koedt, William Masters, Margaret Mead, Kate Millett, the *Our Bodies, Ourselves* health collective and Mary Jane Sherfey, M.D.

For their support and encouragement, we should like to thank June Arnold, Parke Bowman, Charlotte Bunch, Sharon Delano, Beverly Fisher, Helen Merrill, Nancy Myron, Jean Warfield, Jennifer Wyland.

Contents

Introduction 9

Lesbian sex
and lesbian lifestyles 17

A lesbian bibliography 179

Index 189

We dedicate this book on joy to
free women everywhere, but
particularly to those women
who, through the ages, struggled
to make our freedom possible.

Introduction

Lesbianism, in the popular imagination, has been a phenomenon somewhat like China: a vast, sequestered territory at once both terrifying and inviting; a complex weave of the unknown veiled in rites and mysteries arousing both enchantment and fear. Lesbianism, it has been supposed, is that place where one cannot go and return unchanged. Like China, there has been a great wall around the lesbian, rendering her untouchable, silent, invisible to those outside.

China's wall was built by those within; ours has been constructed around us by those without. It makes a prison, not a country; an uneasy encampment, not a people. The wall was built with equal parts of loathing and attraction. It was fixed with the mortar of superstition. Behind the wall has lived for all the long time we call "civilization" a creature of the superstitious impulse: a witch, a contagion. Or else, a vision of unparalleled temptation, a palace of erotic splendor. Never real, never customary, the lesbian's life has been a figment of the imagination.

No amount of empirical observation or rational discourse to the contrary has been able to dispel entirely these unearthly visions of the lesbian, perhaps because, given the nature of heterosexual reality, there is in them a kernel of truth to which the irrational mind still responds. The lesbian is imaged as a monster, of evil or of delight, because she is the synthesis of all threats to the patriarchal sense of male supremacy/female passivity and the reduction of sexual joy within the paradigm to obligation.

The role of the lesbian has been to show the patriarchy what has been scourged from all human life, what has been walled in to suffer, wither and die in all of us: the erotic, that which is normally reduced to no more than systems of penile gratification. The lesbian is what we almost lost entirely: to free her is to find again the meaning of pleasure; to free her is to begin to understand pleasure as an impulse toward freedom.

In 1484 Jacob Sprenger published a treatise on witches entitled *Malleus Maleficarum (The Hammer of the Witches)*. Sprenger's intention was to settle, once and for all, the question of "what women want"—and what should be done about it. His language is antique; the sentiments he expresses are, unfortunately, still fresh:

". . . woman is a wheedling and secret enemy. And that she is more perilous than a snare does not speak of the snare of hunters, but of devils. For men are caught not only through their carnal desires, when they see and hear women. For S. Bernard says: Their face is as a burning wind, and their voice the hissing of serpents: but they also cast wicked spells on countless men and animals. And when it is said that her heart is a net, it speaks of the inscrutable malice which reigns in their hearts. And her hands are as bands for binding; for when they place their hands on a creature to bewitch it, then with the help of the devil they perform their design. To conclude, All witchcraft comes from carnal lust, which is in women insatiable."

". . . *carnal lust, which is in women insatiable*"—fear of women is fear of the erotic. It is unmanly to be fearful. Therefore, that which is feared must be obliterated. But it is impractical to eradicate all women (and make the world safe for the penis), so she who is left must be taught tameness. The lesbian is a woman who refuses to be tamed. She is the emblem of eroticism that resists death-by-socialization.

Those times that have been most phallocentric in temperament have also been, not surprisingly, also most directly brutal in their suppression of the feminine principle, with which erotic variation is

always associated. Typically, such times give rise to parallel political ideologies which give structure as well as outlet to the collective
fear (Sprenger's theological structure was nonetheless political).
The world has called such eras, "militaristic," "puritan," "Nazi,"
"fascist," and they are sincerely loathed by all people of good will.
Good will, however, has not gone to the root of the problem. It has
not taken into account the fear of the female as the organizing sensation beneath the political posture, and it has been blind to the
social and psychological by-products of it: rigid gender polarization,
severely demarcated roles and irrational fear of difference. The Nazi
prescription for women—*Kinder, Kirche, Küche*—is a logical result
of Sprenger's analysis of feminine evil.

Reality means heterosexual reality. That reality's limited purpose
has been to get a penis inside a vagina to produce ejaculation for the
male and a fetus in the woman. The insertion of the penis into the
vagina has described culture, history, business, technology, politics,
war; it has formulated social as well as sexual intercourse: something out there has got to "get fucked." More masculine energy has
gone into justifying this single act, into teaching women to build
their lives around it, into elaborating ritual, symbol, law and taboo
to reinforce it than into any other endeavor—with one single excep-
tion: to limit and control sexual pleasure. The connection between
the two is obvious: heterosexual reality includes the female orgasm
by accident only.

It has been suggested that human urgency to reproduce is the
root of the heterosexual obsession. This, in part, is true. But keeping your [*sic*] woman "barefoot and pregnant" ensures in the first
instance that she will not run away and have a good time and, in the
second, that for a considerable portion of her life she will hardly be
able to actualize her sexuality at all. Once again, Jacob Sprenger's
admonition to the male is newly expressed. In our society, a shoeless
woman in labor is the apotheosis of entrapment and pain. Denied
pleasure, women put their faith in self-denial. For example, by old
(post-menopausal) age, women should have learned that their sexuality is a matter of uterine function; they should have learned too
that when the uterus quits, the rest of their bodies too are a back
number. Post-menopausal women are not supposed to feel sexual.
They are supposed to feel like mothers-in-law, since they are no
longer capable of being mothers.

Heterosexual reality for men is sexual, for women it is largely
reproductive. But need for children alone cannot explain the thou-
sands of years of barbaric repression, of psychological and physical
mutilation, of inchoate hysteria that have greeted the appearance
of lesbianism.

The obverse of woman-hating is man-loving. The function of

heterosexuality as a reproductive ritual is to permit the male to achieve as much distance from the frightening female as possible; and to come close to her only to achieve a child in his own image. We suggest that loathing of female sexuality is stimulated by more than fear of its independent character. There is also in the response to women a strong element of male empathy with male. In recognizing this, we further simplify the definition of heterosexual reality by calling its *emotional* nature *homosexual*. Heterosexuality indicates, therefore, for men as well as women, only a reproductive ritual.

In this light, the lesbian becomes the antithesis of woman. The lesbian is the living rejection of woman-hating. Even more critically she is a living denial of female self-hatred. She is self-love and she loves what is despised. The social prohibitions placed on lesbianism are formulated from this understanding. Her own self-love, her love for women, could become contagious. If men began to love women, as lesbians do, if women began to love women, as lesbians do, empires (at least) would crumble. Sexual joy would replace sexual fear.

The argument against eroticism has been refined by every patriarchal culture hero until it has emerged as *credo*: man is born what he is, but woman must be forced to become what she must be.

Jean-Jacques Rousseau (in *Emile: On Education*), while allowing that "man" may be "A creature often vicious and always faulty" he is still man and must be served: A woman

"should learn to submit to injustice and to suffer the wrongs inflicted on her by her husband without complaint; she must he gentle for her own sake, not his. Bitterness and obstinacy only multiply the sufferings of the wife and the misdeeds of the husband."

"Natural" Woman (to be an appropriate counterpart to Rousseau's Natural Man) must learn masochism.

"As a general rule, a modest woman seldom desires any sexual gratification for herself"; thus William Acton urges frigidity upon Victorian women. Hegel would make them stupid: "Women can, of course, be educated, but their minds are not adapted to the higher sciences, philosophy, or certain of the arts." Schopenhauer meditates on sexual intercourse: "It is an action of which in cold reflection one generally thinks with dislike and in a lofty mood with loathing." And all agree to behave like God, who, of course, gave the first instructions on how to make a female into a "woman." To Eve, God passes on the outline of her future, and the future of all her daughters: "I will greatly multiply thy sorrow and thy conception. . . ."

Sigmund Freud's experience with women—and with what women want—was almost as limited as God's. But Freud goes further than God. To ensure conception, Freud advocates rape: "Nature has paid less careful attention to the demands of the female function than to those of masculinity . . . the achievement of the biological aim is entrusted to the aggressiveness of the male, and is to some extent independent of the cooperation of the female."

In the midst of this lengthy onslaught against a woman's body and a woman's mind, where is the lesbian? "To my knowledge," said Queen Victoria, "lesbianism does not exist." That is to say, female sexuality independent of the uterus and the penis does not exist.

Lesbian: it is a word so freighted with cultural, historical and sexual content that heretofore one dared not speak the thing it names. It has been a secret. It is like no other word in the language: it cannot enter ordinary speech; the word, and what it represents, must remain unspoken. To name a thing is to give it life. To have life is to have power. The man on the street calls the lesbian a "female faggot." The more sophisticated call her an "invert," a "queer," "pervert," "dyke," "sapphist," none of which gives life. Indeed, they operate to conceal life, conjuring up visions of pseudo-maleness and in so doing cancelling associations with the feminine.

The story of civilization has been the story of the phallus: its identity, its behavior on land and sea, its worship, in particular its peculiar property of always being co-present with superior brain cells. The story of woman in this civilization has been the story of her relationship to the phallus. She has been the sub-plot added to introduce intrigue, conflict and (as Simone de Beauvoir stated as early as 1949) something "other" than the male norm.

A growing number of scholars, like Robert Graves, insist it wasn't always this way. They have shown that male domination, with its accompanying myths of intellectual and sexual superiority, is a relatively new mark on the face of the earth. Words like "matri-archy," "gynocracy," "Amazon" have re-entered the language. Whether there is real pre-historical fact behind them is not as important as the hope they give for the future. Like the word "les-bian" they serve to show us human possibility. Because we have been nameless, it is particularly important to lesbians that history- and culture-bearing words be named. Without a word, a thing does not socially, culturally, politically exist.

Once, the historical story goes, there was no word for "father," for "husband," for "wife." It goes without saying there were no "in-law" words. The universe was imagined as a great mother. Her rep-resentatives were ruling queens. The stories were of the queen and her lovers; of the queen and her children. Any five-star general can understand why this history was obliterated: you cannot accomplish a thorough-going takeover of a people before you cause that people to forget the language, arts, religion, stories, myths that gave them identity, that made them real. First, you must teach them to become something they are not and teach them to feel shame for what they have been. In time they will forget their past.

Female amnesia is the pre-condition of what passes for human history. Women are only now regaining consciousness. Before consciousness the lesbian was myth. As myth, she exploded into symbol and encapsulated all that men fear about women—and more: she has been used, as dream, to personify loss and guilt. As nightmare, she is our rage and grief over what we miss in life—the full meaning of the erotic.

Lesbian sexuality, quite literally, is about *re*-creation. It is the interface of mind, body, spirit. It is non-economic. It is for pleasure. Its materialization is in poetic knowledge of the life of the flesh. It is equal, because women together are equals and vehemence against the lesbian is vehemence against democracy as well as eroticism.

Women are multi-orgasmic and men are not; that physiological difference, though it is an expression primarily of sexual energy, carries over into different perceptions of their wider energy by women and men. To be a man is to feel a limitation on energy. To be a man means to feel that life is a question of either/or: there is either work or play, either intellectual or sexual opportunity. One can either make love or make war. Men understand that they cannot have or be everything. No matter what the splendor of the ejaculation, when it is over the energy that whetted it is gone and must slowly be built up again. To be a woman though is to have seemingly limitless energy. She greets the dawn; she reproduces, feeds, nurtures, clothes; she scrubs the floor; she becomes a captain of industry—or hits the street to demand the chance to become one. Even God and Freud wonder at her capacity to love, and at her ability to survive without love. Her energy is always available.

The discovery (or re-discovery) of female physiological fact has been the greatest challenge to masculinist order the world has ever experienced. Women discovered that they had a clitoris; next, they felt what it could do; then, they understood that the clitoris is unique in the human anatomy, that its sole function is to give pleasure. Female pleasure (as Jacob Sprenger understood) is without limitation, either orgasmically or in the production of work and art. At the same time, woman recognized that the penis is an accessory to sexual pleasure; at worst, an impediment. Women observed that a penis is easily exhausted and that tongues, fingers, vibrators, water sprays, thighs, arms, legs, feet, toes—and another clitoris—are not. On the basis of this recognition, many women have learned that it is easier to produce work, as well as love, with a woman than it is with a man; that sometimes it is easier to raise children with another woman that it is with a man.

Gradually, as man did before her, woman has begun to dream a culture, a civilization, based on the behavior of herself in orgasm—

a system of radiating circles encompassing spirit as well as body. She has, at last, learned from her flesh her meaning: what she *is* rather than what she is conventionally forced to become.

It is simplest—and least misleading—to call this new creation lesbian. In so doing, we dispose of the lies that have encrusted the meaning of "woman" and give her, woman, choice. The "great wall" falls apart and we see in full daylight what was in our midst all along in all guises—the spinster, the housewife, the artist, the teacher, the executive, the athlete, the politician, the dreamer, daughter, wife, mother, mother-in-law, sister, grandmother: a lesbian. Charlotte Bunch, a leading theoretician of the new feminism, sums the situation up very simply: "A woman is not free to be anything unless she is *also* free to be a lesbian."

In writing this book, we have released what all of us forget at our peril: that whereas the mind decides, the body defines.

"Gradually...woman has begun to dream a culture, a civilization, based on the behavior of herself in orgasm — a system of radiating circles encompassing spirit as well as body. She has, at last, learned from her flesh her meaning: what she is rather than what she is conventionally forced to become."

Alcohol and sex Better be prepared to choose which you want more of, for they work in inverse proportion. A little alcohol may permit a lot of sex, especially at first, when both of you may need some loosening of inhibitions. A lot of alcohol will deaden your nerve endings, making response extremely difficult if not impossible. Two women who persist in trying to make love after heavy drinking are far more apt to end up with sore genitalia than anything resembling orgasm.

We're not talking about a little champagne with a festive breakfast in bed, or a cocktail or two before dinner; we're talking about washing down a whole batch of booze and then falling into bed with amorous ideas. Better save them for the morning.

As for alcoholism, it's been our experience—both clinically and through personal observation—that lesbians are not afflicted at a rate any greater than the general population. When heavy drinking assumes problem proportions, it seems to be a reaction to stress less associated with lesbianism than with the demands of a competitive, acquisitive business world. The image of a lonely, middle-aged lesbian hunched over endless scotches may reflect the outside world's view that gays can't be happy, but it is simply not accurate.

Anatomy of sex Organs such as the ovaries and the uterus are for procreation, not sex. The genitals are the means to the former and the key to the latter, which is why we limit our discussion to them alone.

To inspect her genitals without a mirror a woman would have to be a contortionist, but propping herself up with pillows in front of a mirror she has both hands free to separate her lips.

First off, there is an enormous variation in shape, size, positioning, and the general configuration of women's genitalia. Reaching down from the uppermost section, at the level of the pubic bone, is the clitoral shaft. Then you encounter the hood of the clitoris, which can be retracted for better viewing of that relatively small but powerful mass of erectile tissue that gives you most of your jollies. The larger folds of tissue more or less surrounding this whole area are the outer or major lips (*labia*). Farther down, around the vaginal opening, are the inner or minor lips. The whole area is the *vulva* and the skin separating vulva from anus is the *perineum*.

Aside from these guidelines there is not a great deal to say except to repeat that no two women are built exactly the same, as the active lesbian soon discovers. The color and shape of the tissue— not to mention the amount and configuration of surrounding pubic hair—vary considerably. But, of course, the basic equipment is all there and, as is elaborated throughout this book, learning about your lover's entire body is the fun of lovemaking.

We might add that enlightened women gynecologists are playing an active role in educating their patients about anatomy—even, for example, having the woman use a mirror to view her own cervix when the vagina is dilated for an examination. Women who may for one reason or another be shy about inspecting their own sexual equipment may well find that consulting a sympathetic gynecologist can help ease their anxiety.

Anus This highly sensitive portion of everyone's anatomy has, in the literature of sexuality and in the poetry of many cultures, been associated with flower images—"little rose," for example, or "an opening at the base of a flower"—to suggest its potential for sexual delight. It is often neglected by lesbians and non-gays to their disadvantage.

Except for the clitoris (which is there for nothing but pleasure) all portions of the human anatomy have more than one function and the "secondary" function is always sexual: tongues speak and taste and can bring a lover to orgasm; breasts can nourish an infant and connect with the clitoris in an almost electric charge of excitement; there is almost nothing a set of agile fingers cannot do. While the anus is almost always the last bit of the anatomy to come out of the sexual closet in lesbian lovemaking, as a locus for erotic abandonment in women it is second only to the clitoris.

There are two basic methods by which lesbians commonly approach anal intercourse—but these, and all variations on them, *must*, if tried, be accompanied with gentleness and preceded by a state of sexual excitement. Even then, some form of lubrication (it can be as ordinary as butter) is desirable.

With your lover lying on her stomach, you start by massaging her buttocks gently, then more deeply (this can be preceded by a back massage—see *Backs* and *Massage*). You begin to part her buttocks and slip a hand in and out of her cleft, brushing the anus lightly. When you come to concentrate on the anus, your initial gestures should be no more than light, but deliberate, touches. Her anus should be responding to your touch with involuntary contractions and this is your clue that the time is right for entry. Slowly, with the middle (and lubricated) finger, you enter her, always monitoring her response. Sometimes she may want no more than part of a finger inside; at other times she may crave its full length. You should always follow her movements, gently alternating light thrusts and circular rubbing—this alone can bring some women to orgasm, especially if they have a pillow also rubbing against the clitoris. While one hand is stimulating the anus, however, the other hand may be working on her vagina and/or on her clitoris. This is best effected by letting her press her open labia against three fingers

(middle, ring and pinkie) while the index operates inside the vagina; a vibrator or dildo can take over the fingerwork.

Face-to-face anal sex is a little more difficult for the active partner to effect; but, with practice, equally rewarding. The face-to-face position is usually started and accompanied by vaginal and clitoral activity. In this instance, the middle finger enters the anus while the index of the same hand strokes the clitoris and enters the vagina.

Some women find it easier to use the thumb than the index.

Very few lesbians in fact like anything as large as a dildo inserted into their anus, but beware of the insertion of small objects—they do get lost, as any hospital will tell you. It really comes down to fingers and, if you like them, dildos. In all cases, however, objects that have entered the anus must *not* subsequently enter the vagina until they have been washed with soap and water.

Aphrodisiacs An aphrodisiac is anything that induces or heightens sensuality; the greatest aphrodisiac of all is your imagination as you build a rich fantasy around what exactly is going to happen, with whom and in what circumstances. An aphrodisiac, therefore, is anything that turns you on: lying naked in the hot sun feeling your flesh melt, a glass of wine, a (shared) joint, a love note, music. But any aphrodisiac only works when used with delicacy: while a little wine, for instance, will inflame desire, too much will diminish performance. And the hot sun, while it opens you sensually, can put you to sleep. The selection of aphrodisiacs is a minor refinement in the cosmos of lesbian sexuality, but it is an activity that especially rewards lovers who have passed through the early stages of ecstasy and have grown too automatic in their lovemaking.

Après-midi d'une lesbienne The afternoon of a love affair: that time between two lovers when the glitter of being in love is dulled and erodes into routine; the time that comes when you realize that you are used to each other, when it seems that there are no new erotic nuances you can discover and share; when both of you are most vulnerable to a stranger with her promise of new adventures; that time which the wise prepare for and the inexperienced are shocked by: you have, perhaps, vowed eternal love—it is unimaginable that you can ever get enough of one another; or you have started the relationship less romantically, more rationally: you will love each other until you love each other no longer—and then behave in a civilized fashion about it.

Rationality, however, seldom affects the conditions of being in love, loving or lusting. It is, therefore, particularly important to be aware from the beginning that the afternoon of love will inevitably happen—but that you will have a choice, in this as in all other matters of love, about what you will do with it. There are seldom any external supports (such as heterosexuals have) for a lesbian relationship, other than those individual couples make for themselves. The essential factor that makes the difference between suffering and avoiding pain is *awareness of choice*, the knowledge that you can control the events of your love life and not be overwhelmed; awareness, too, that love between women can take many forms and reach many dimensions.

You have reached the afternoon when you are doing the same thing in bed every time you make love together, when you always make love at the same time of the day or night—or, out of boredom, you are not making love at all. You have reached the afternoon when, with her fingers inside you, you are mentally balancing your checkbook; you have reached the afternoon when it doesn't matter to you how long she will be gone because you are certain she'll come back eventually. You have reached the afternoon when there is no longer any surprise, tension or expectation of newness in your relationship. When this happens—and it will—you can choose among the following: give up sex, or use it only for physical relief; continue to be with each other as a security against loneliness, enjoy dining together, movie-going together, playing together, even sleeping together, but finding sex in other places (this choice works only if you have both honestly agreed that the arrangement is mutually satisfactory, and if your outside lovers also accept the situation before you go to bed with them); recognize that while there is love there is hope for sexual renewal. Stop waiting for inspiration to return and start creating it deliberately. Renew the pleasure of courtship: bring her a little gift or some flowers. The surprised smile on her face may be just the aphrodisiac you need. Turn on some music instead of the television; open some wine instead of the evening paper. Leave a very sexual suggestion taped to the bathroom mirror, or write out an explicit account of your favorite sexual fantasy and pin it to her pillow. Buy a vibrator and let her watch you use it on yourself. This way you may turn your afternoon into the best sexual experience the two of you have enjoyed. But if nothing works, if it's really over, remember that you're a lesbian—and one of the most important liberties you enjoy as a lesbian is that you're as free to go as you are to come.

Armpits The authors of our straight counterpart, *The Joy of Sex*, strenuously object to deodorants and to shaving. They complain of the "disappointments" of a "mouthful of aluminum chloride" and chastise women because "some of the nicest of them [i.e. women] still . . . chop off their armpit hair."

Well, each to his, or her, own taste (no pun intended). Sexy as armpit hair may be to play with in bed, its appearance drooping down over a sleeveless summer sheath or the bra of a bikini strikes many women (very much including lesbians) as strikingly unesthetic. As for smells, perhaps this is just one more area where women differ from men. Most women discover some odor charac-

teristic of the woman they love and associate it with sexual excitement. In particular, most women enjoy the musky scent of their
partner's—as well as their own—secretions. But rare is the woman
who will wax poetic over the odor (or taste) of armpit sweat. In fact,
it's frequently described as a real turn-off and a cause for the swift
assumption of some other position.

Therefore—most especially for those whom our straight counterpart calls "the unfortunates who sweat profusely"—some pretty careful thought should be given to the risks of not using underarm deodorants. As for shaving, try to base your decision on what is most comfortable and/or appealing for you (and your lover) and not on "fad"—whether the fad stems from altered attitudes of men *or* exhortations of feminists for whom the presence or absence of body hair has taken on new meanings.

Arousal Arousal is usually a tingly, urgent, driving sense of receptivity with the heightened expectation of moving to orgasm. But not always.

One lesbian describes arousal as accompanying an accomplished soprano in a Fauré song. There the union is sensual, not sexual. Indeed, women's capacity to translate experiences into inward sensuality is without bounds. Candlelight, a meaningful glance across a room, the first warm breeze of June become internalized as part of a woman's feeling of romance. We think this may account for the intensity of lesbian love; the combination of similar temperaments and similarity of sensual experience is not duplicated in any other sexual union.

Lesbians often enjoy arousal for itself. When it leads to sex and orgasm, all well and good, but just staying there can sometimes be equally satisfying, and that's a fact two women in love have no difficulty in understanding.

Backs The number of back rubs given and received in women's dormitories is an index to the amount of lesbian erotic feeling in the atmosphere at that time. For the straight, the uninitiated or the repressed, the back rub is the beginning and the end of sensual expression, but for the full-blown lesbian the back rub is one of the smoothest, most sensual entries into lovemaking. Further, it combines three important elements that form the basis for successful lovemaking: it profoundly relaxes and opens the body, it stimulates it and it conveys a message of caring and tenderness.

If your lover is too tired for sex at the end of a heavy day, she usually means that she is too tense to even imagine relaxing enough to respond. You will however almost invariably find that once the back's tension is smoothed and drained away, the sexually essential parts of the body will wake up refreshed and ready to go.

First you undress her; put her in a lukewarm shower for five minutes (a hot bath at this point will send her straight to sleep); take her out, briskly rub her dry and stretch her out, backside up, on the bed. If she has occasional twinges of lower back pain she will be more comfortable with a pillow beneath her pelvis. After you have undressed you straddle her buttocks, but don't sit or put your full weight on her; your knees and thighs should support you. Her head should be against the mattress or resting on a thin pillow, her arms should be flat by her sides.

Since the day's cumulative anxieties and strains tend to deposit themselves in the shoulders, sometimes to a painful extent, start by leaning forward and working them both, at first lightly and caressingly, but with increasingly deeper pressure coming from the heels

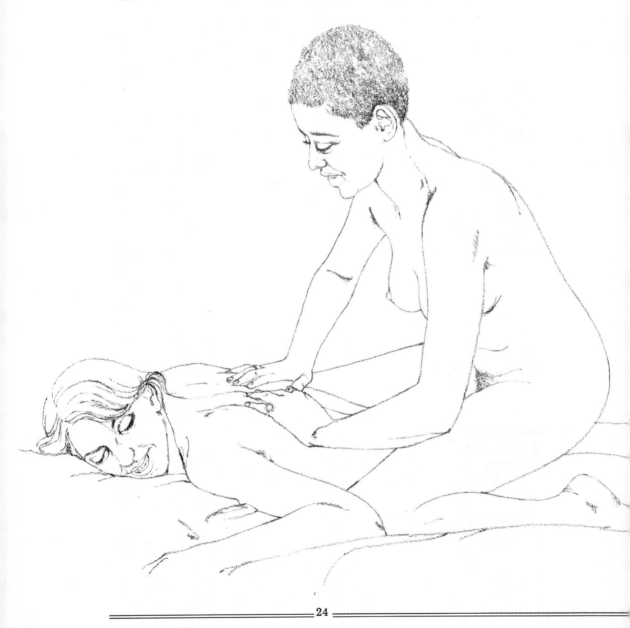

of your hands. Push and rub hard into the muscles: your goal is to overwhelm the armor of tension resisting you. Sometimes this is so intense you may have to ball your hands into fists and pummel the shoulder area. Gradually move beneath the shoulder blades and onto the rib cage, pressing and rubbing with your palms flattened against her body. At intervals, return to the shoulders; at these times introduce a squeezing, lifting motion. Then return to the back proper, giving particular attention to each little knob of the spine with the tips of your fingers. The lower back, the "tailbone," should come last, and her sensitivity in this area should be your guide to how much pressure you exert. Here, use your fingers (the three middle ones) as if they were a long-handled spoon with which you're whipping a bowl of cream with light, rapid movements. If she is entirely relaxed (and she should be by this point), her whole body should jiggle in rhythm with your fingers.

Keeping your hands lubricated with a lotion during the back rub not only facilitates their swim across her back but also increases the sensory content of the experience for her. Do not, however, pour lotion onto her back—the shock of something cold will produce quite the wrong effect. Rubbing the lotion into your hands first will warm it up and transmit both silkiness and your body heat.

The crucial difference between a back rub and a lesbian back rub is in the matter of your ultimate goal: sex. So while you're rubbing out the back's exhaustion, you can occasionally let your fingers insinuate themselves around to her front, cupping her breasts, teasing a nipple. You can use your mouth too and surprise her with a well-aimed kiss on her tailbone. You can run your tongue, instead of your fingers, up and down her spine. As a finale you can stroke her buttocks, and when you know she's ready, without missing a beat, you can spread her (by now utterly compliant) legs and begin making love at either the anus or the vagina. If she has a pillow beneath her pelvis you can even reach her clitoris.

Bars Lesbians don't go to gay bars primarily to drink. Every lesbian who goes to gay bars does so because she knows that the people around her are like her. She knows, too, that these strangers take her sexuality for granted; that the men (if the bar is mixed) won't try to pick her up; that the women are potentially friends or lovers; that, with her own kind, she is safe from the outside world's molestation.

It's a sorry judgment on that "outside world" that it provides hardly any alternative to these typically shabby, typically fly-by-night places with their emphasis on drinking and drink-hustling. The ambience of any community's lesbian bar, from its carpentry and decor to its drink prices and toilet facilities, is an index to that community's attitude toward the lesbians in its midst. But lesbians go to their bars, no matter what they are like, for the bars are still a reliable bulwark against isolation and loneliness; the only places that are consistently various, where any lesbian may, without invitation, enter and find the enchanted stranger. Despite recent lesbian political activity which has led to bar "alternatives"—poetry readings, dances, conferences—the bars are still the place of the enchanted stranger. And lesbians are still prepared to pay her price. Poetry readings, no matter how moving, are no substitute for the slow grind on a pitch-dark dance floor; conferences are work, not romance; politically sponsored dances are about sisterhood, not sex. And all of these alternative events shut down before the bars do: the lonely lesbian has more time to wait there and hope; the happy lesbian has more time to play.

Bars for lesbians, despite some heavy sexual overtones, are not what they are for gay men. They are not principally about direct sexual availability. In many respects, the difference between the male homosexual's use of his bar and the lesbian's use of hers is a microcosm of the difference between male and female sexuality. Alone in the bar, the lesbian waits to "meet someone," but that meeting usually means more to both her body and her imagination than an anonymous sexual encounter. So it is unfortunate that the scared-to-death lesbian frequently adopts macho habits or (their opposite) timid-mouse habits to cure her aloneness. "Meeting someone" can be tricky or simple, depending mostly—as in other things—on one's attitudes toward doing it. Slamming the door open and stalking to the bar where you conduct a furtive ten-minute check for the love of your life is not the road to success any more than the chain-smoking crouch over a glass of beer.

There is still a horrifyingly large number of lesbians who think that in a bar the proper approach to a woman they admire is a slap on her beautiful ass. But hard and deliberate conditioning has trained many women into near-paralysis. In response, lesbians often adopt the grossly inappropriate habits of men to make moves toward each other. A genuinely female, a genuinely lesbian move toward another woman is most gracefully accomplished with an invitation to dance, where custom gives licence as talk, at first, frequently does not. "Will you dance?" you ask, and smile—even though your heart is pounding visibly through your shirt. The invitation to dance can be a euphemism among lesbians for many other invitations, but mostly it means: can I get together with you for a little while, move a little apart from you and watch you move? And then can we talk and get to know each other? Hours later, or weeks later, if there is personal mesh, sex may come of it as well as friendship or love. The answer to the invitation, of course, may be no—but don't assume it's your magenta snakeskin cowboy boots or the cigar clenched between your teeth that's turning her off. It's possible that she's up next for the pool game; it's possible that her notoriously possessive lover has just stepped into the john. Or (entirely in your boots' favor) she's throwing aside all the rules and just hopes you'll sit and talk to her. And it's always worth it to take that chance: the love of your life (or of your winter or spring) might not have learned to dance because, where she comes from, dancing means encounters with the boys. But even if you don't dance and you're not ready yet to learn how in the midst of all that energetic lust a lesbian bar dance floor generates, just watching women move is by no means boring. Certainly it beats sitting at home and watching straight couples get it together on TV. And the spillover of music and movement from the floor to your table may create exactly the urgent context you both need to get the conversation off her bull terrier and your fourteen-year-old Persian and on to what you're doing for dinner the next night; or even (but this is rare in a first encounter) whether it's her place or yours tonight.

The straight-and-narrow advocates are, of course, entirely serving their best interests when, in preventing same-sex dancing, they hope to prevent same-sex sex. In a small space filled with women where there is just enough light to keep the sober from stumbling over tables and which is booming with sound that is little more than pelvic rhythms, the lesbian displays her body, shows what her body can do, invites another body to consider joining hers in the dance that dancing mimes. Gay bars will always be imperfect environments for love of woman for woman to begin, but they are the most enduring temples of foreplay we have.

Basics   There are several different ways in which the basics of sex and love can be viewed.

Knowledge of equipment: People who want to sexualize their relationship will usually stumble across ways to achieve it. It helps, of course, to have a clear idea of where things are and what does what. Information of this sort can be found under *Anatomy of sex* and the headings describing particular parts.

Knowledge of procedures: This is the how of assuming different positions and the familiarity with techniques for kissing, fucking, sucking, rubbing, and all the many other activities women engage in while making love.

Another view: Basics can also be interpreted as those constituents without which making love is simply having sex. That is, the capacity for intimacy which, unlocked by the desire to share, involves relinquishing control needs, fully accepting the other as a self in her own right, wanting to please, gratify, be pleased and be gratified;

in short, caring about another human being so that she is not just your lover but also the woman you love.

It is that sense of engagement between two people that converts having sex into making love. There is a profound difference, and human beings' capacity to recognize and experience that difference may very well be at the root of all creative efforts to celebrate the combination of emotions we call love. It could be that difficulty in recognizing and experiencing that difference is the principal reason for people seeking psychotherapy or other counsel.

But given that a lesbian, just as any other well glued together person, both recognizes and experiences the difference, how does she express it in sexual activity?

Women, so goes the popular opinion, are more tender, more giving, more given to cuddling and nuzzling than men. Some bisexuals (that way either by proclivity or happenstance) question this generalization—particularly gay men and gay women who have made it together. It is all in the person, they say, not in the gender. This is not an unreasonable surmise if you consider that a good half of what psychology used to call "intrapsychic" is clearly a reflection of social, economic and cultural pressures. Is the "average" man, for example, less "nice"—that is, more the snarling beast—than the "average" woman? Or could it be that his socialization as a flannel-suited Tarzan taught him that wham-bam-thank-you-ma'am is normal male sexuality?

Be that as it may this book is more about hows than whys. Whether women are naturally more complex in their sexual responses than men and whether men's response is more "like putting a quarter in a vending machine" is not our concern—except as this sort of typecasting limits the pleasure women are able to imagine for themselves as lesbians. Lesbians have a great psychological advantage: there's hardly one alive who doesn't believe she's better at making love to a woman than a man is.

Beds Probably as a result of today's less inhibited mores, bed is less the place where lesbians (or anyone else) make love. Still, in all, it remains the most common site for exploration and consummation.

As with so many things, extremes are to be avoided. Too soft is not only unhealthy for the spinal column but it also overyields to create crevices and valleys that can trap parts of the body that ought to be accessible to strokes and kisses. It's also difficult to bounce and play on too soft a bed. On the other hand, too hard a bed presents its own hazards. For example, prolonged sucking on a bed with not enough give for you or your partner can result in pain rather like that induced by a whiplash injury to the neck.

A sort of medium-hard/medium-soft surface is best—enough give for comfort, but enough support for bounding about. Good-quality foam rubber of five-inch thickness, placed on a flat pine support, makes an excellent bed for lovemaking. Such a bed can be purchased cheaply or made at even less expense if you're handy. This kind of bed also offers you a wider choice of width, height, length—even unusual shapes—than commercial mattresses on box springs. It is also easy to carry, so you can move it into the living-room if you so wish.

If your bed has no headboard it's wise to place it against a wall so that with the addition of thick but comfortable cushions you have something to lean against as you eat breakfast in bed. Speaking of breakfast in bed, it's important to keep in mind that your bed will be used for many activities only peripherally related to sex and sleeping —playful games like wrestling, hide-and-seek under the covers, friendly pillow fights, and various versions of "let's pretend." So avoid nearby overhead shelving and sharp-cornered tables.

Big toe There is no portion of your body that is not capable of arousal or that cannot be used to arouse a lover. Toe-sucking (clean toe-sucking) is one of the more sensational erotic practices, but in form is simplicity itself. This is how it can most be enjoyed if you want to engage.

You can grasp her feet firmly; separate her toes with your fingers, and as though they were lollipops suck each toe thoroughly in turn. The effect is explosive: it's as if the nerves of the toes were directly connected with the clitoris. A variation on this practice is to leave one hand free to work the clitoris and vagina while the other hand and the mouth stimulate the toes.

The big toe, by contrast, can be transformed into an active agent and be tireless at fucking in a way the fingers are not. Unless you prop yourself up on your elbows between her legs, a bed is usually too short to practice toe-fucking, so it's out of bed and onto the floor. Before beginning, make sure your feet are clean and your toes well manicured with no pernicious hang-nails: the aim is to produce moans, not shrieks. Both stretch out, hips to toes. Using both feet you part her thighs and begin rubbing her bush with the ball or heel of your foot. Using the toes, you open her labia and begin to stimulate her clitoris with the big toe. Gradually shift to your side, propping yourself up, if necessary, on an elbow and slip your big toe down around and into her vagina. As the big toe thrusts, the other four toes will be almost reflexively working against the inner labia and clitoris. Of all sexual practices, toe-fucking is most amenable to simultaneous indulgence instead of taking turns: with only a foot engaged, the rest of the body is free to move to orgasm at its own pace. Some women, however, prefer to masturbate with a hand or a dildo while they are toe-fucking their partner—or simply wait for their turn.

In more restaurants than would care to be mentioned, toe-fucking is an unannounced item on the menu. All this fearless variation seems to require is a table for two out of the mainstream of diners, a

reasonably long tablecloth and candlelight—very little candlelight. And, of course, one shoe on and one shoe off. For the exceedingly liberated, toe-fucking is a means also of making love simultaneously to two women who will most likely be further stimulating each other as your feet perform.

Bisexuality Now that the essentially bisexual nature of human-kind is accepted as fact, the only thing left for concern is what one does with the information. If wanton lasciviousness is your bag, this era of AC–DC liberation is the perfect cultural ambience for doubling your pleasure. But then, as we've said elsewhere, having sex is not really the focus of this book. Making love is.

Very few gay people, men or women, are absolutely incapable of having sex with someone of the opposite gender. Even fewer have not, with varying degrees of success in the sense of achieving orgasm or pleasure at least, done so, though there may well be a change in this pattern among younger lesbians whose understanding of and commitment to feminism precludes "submitting" to a male. There are several explanations or rationales: experimentation, societal pressure and physical pleasure (it is not in the least rare for lesbians to enjoy penetration, for which a penis can serve as well as other objects, nor for gay men from time to time to revel in the sensations of fucking a vagina rather than other orifices).

But where does that leave love (as in lovemaking)? Is it possible for a person to be equally attracted to members of either sex, and hence to love either?

Yes.

The problem is that, even among swingers, most people swing one way or the other. That is, while "all people are bisexual" most people adopt, fall into, or—best of all—choose a preference. That tends to leave the real bisexual out in the cold. Damned if you do, damned if you don't. Straights can tag you as "queer," gays can say you are unwilling to come out.

Straightforward word of advice: be true to yourself, and honest with people. If you, a woman, fall in love with another woman you are being both true and honest when you act upon that love and enjoy the sensual pleasures you share. If the relationship develops and grows, your bisexuality—openly admitted and just as openly accepted—adds but one more dimension to the liaison: your choice is not just among all women but among all *people*.

Bisexuality should never be used as a weapon. If you say to a lover: "Look, I'm just as turned on by men as I am by women and, just think, out of the whole world, I love you," you are taking unfair advantage. Similarly, if you are not exactly dedicatedly bisexual, but occasionally like to screw with men, make certain that your partner knows that this is an aspect of your personality (or a physical need you sense from time to time) but that it does not diminish your love for her, your enjoyment of her sexuality or your ranking her first in your priorities.

Biting Biting suggests a need both to devour and be devoured—if I eat you up, you'll be inside me; if you eat me up I'll be inside you. Not too many lesbians seem to be caught up with the idea of exercising that much control over someone they love. Nor are that many lesbians turned on by the notion of hurting or being hurt—sadomasochism may be in vogue for gay men, but not for lesbians.

So for "biting" read gentle nibbling. The mouth opens to a wider and wider extent, in tempo with responses, and the teeth edge against, circle around or cautiously close up and down upon the site. Earlobes, the juncture of neck and shoulder, breasts and nipples, the juncture of torso and thighs, and the whole genital area are for most women highly responsive spots. But the whole body is worth exploration—the skin itself is an organ, and one of enormous sensitivity. Biting can be, and generally is, part of a lovemaking repertoire that includes tonguing, stroking and blowing.

Be especially cautious about nibbling the clitoris—or, for that matter, any other highly sensitive part—once you're both near orgasm. In thrashing about, your partner can sustain a bite injury even if you've not actively bitten. At orgasm your jaws can go into spasm, trapping your lover painfully between your teeth. Not only are human bites extremely painful, they're also dangerous. If you should accidently be badly bitten (enough to bring blood) be sure to seek medical advice. And don't be embarrassed to say what happened; the physician is there to treat your wound, not to evaluate your sex life.

Blowing *Not* a blow job, but an acknowledgement of the erotic fact that warm wet skin is outrageously aroused by warm wet currents of air: her armpits, her bush, the outer labia, around the ears, her navel, beneath the hang of her breasts and on her nipples, especially if the blowing is punctuated by quick darts of the tongue or light nips of the teeth. Do not blow into the vagina or ears; light breathing into the ears is all that's required for arousal—more than light breathing will deafen her. Experiment with distances, but keep in mind that the closer your mouth to her skin the more pointed and direct the airstream should be. One of the most effective warm-up acts before lovemaking requires only an ordinary hairdryer with ribbons and feathers attached to

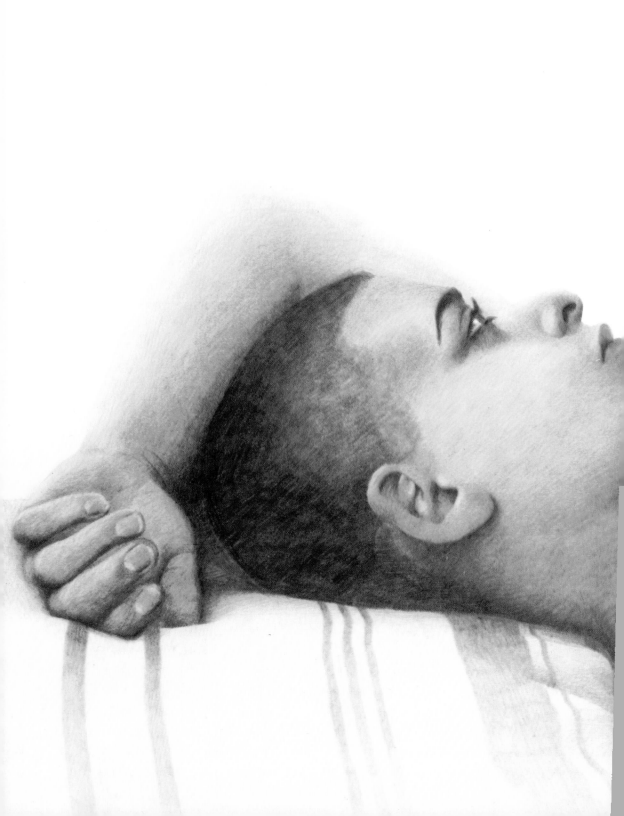

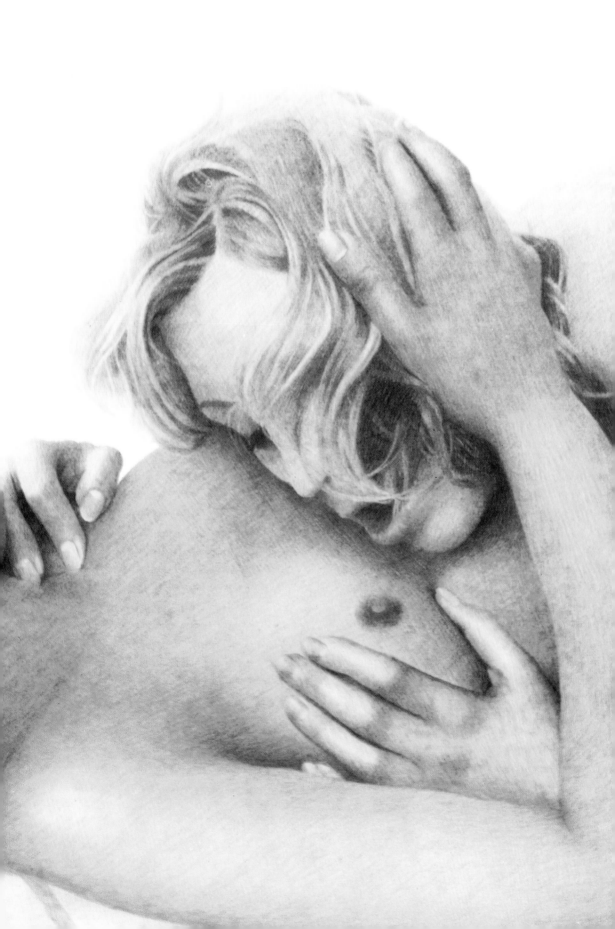

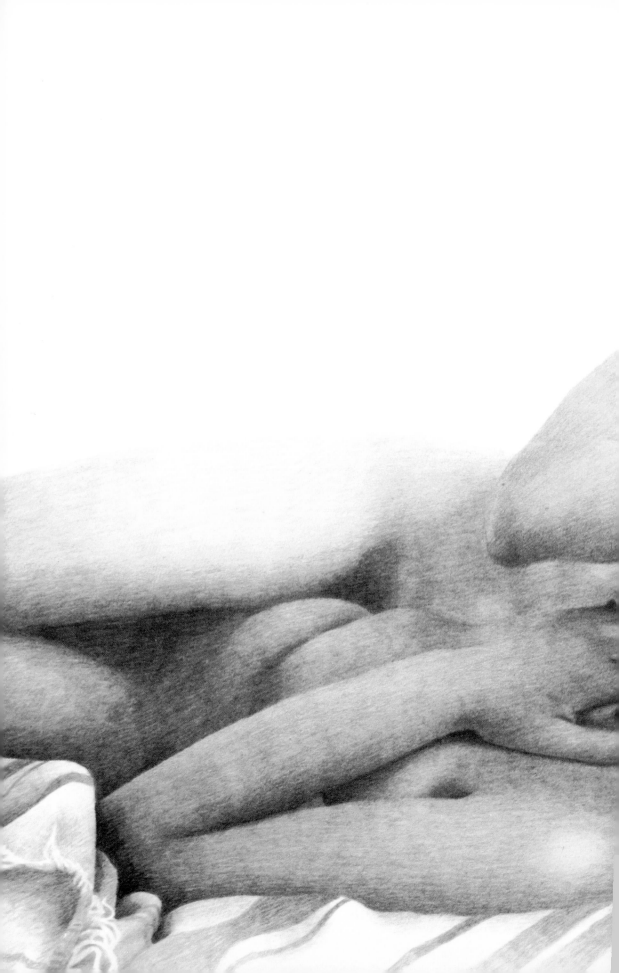

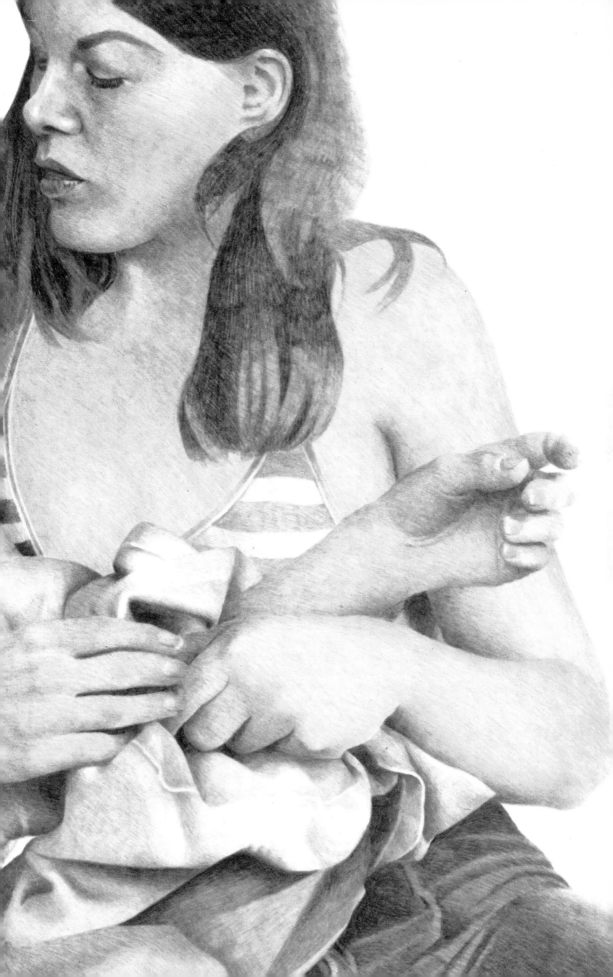

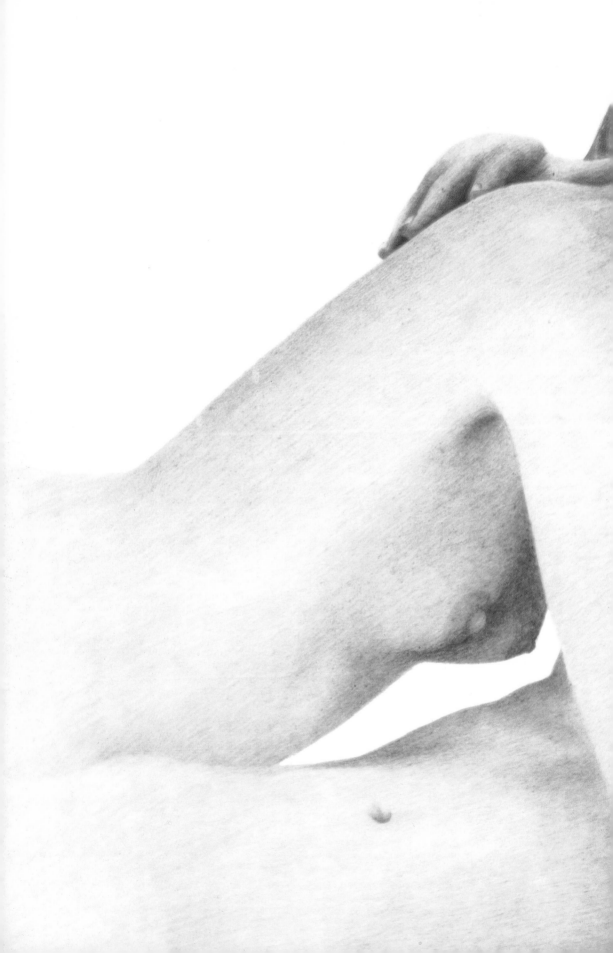

the nozzle. With the temperature of the dryer set on warm, you spread her labia open with your free hand and let the air and its feathery embellishments play against her clitoris. This technique frequently arouses almost to orgasm, and if your fingers are active during the blowing process, it almost invariably achieves it.

Bondage Contrary to the persistent but utterly false myth—"Did you see that middle-aged woman trying to seduce that college girl?" or "Wait till that kid grows up and finds out she has to beat off her queer mother"—lesbians, like women in general, tend not to share male rape fantasies, which are often acted out in scenes of bondage.

On the other hand, if two women are able to overcome their repugnance for methods that have a strong pull toward aggression, playing rough, dominance and submission they may discover that the experience of orgasm can be electrifyingly heightened by bondage. As with so many other things, attitude is the key. If either of you finds the idea in the least distasteful, better forgo the attempt. Another essential is that each of you must thoroughly trust the other. For most women, this will mean being "in love," feeling that you know your lover extremely well, wanting to share experiences and being mutually interested in broadening your sexual repertoire.

The whole point of bondage is to restrain one person from active participation; both the muscular and the emotional effects of this restraint increase sexual excitement and can lead to a sharply heightened orgasm. The bondee need not immediately be the recipient. Her lover may induce an exquisite build-up to the point of aching for contact by masturbating to orgasm in front of the bound partner.

Since fewer and fewer lesbians own beds with head- and footboards, let alone four posters (probably because thick slabs of foam rubber on broad wooden bases offer such good surfaces for lovemaking), staking your partner out spreadeagle fashion may pose some problems. With a little ingenuity doorknobs, the underpinnings of the bed, immovable objects on the floor nearby or the steel frame of a convertible couch may do if your bed doesn't have anchor points.

Unless you and your lover are into leather, or strappings commercially available at sex shops, clothesline probably works best—although items from the wardrobe (bathrobe sashes, stockings, soft belts) may be a turn-on. Whatever you use, be sure it's not going to bruise and be sure it can be untied in a hurry in case of panic, cramps or any sudden physical problem.

Each wrist and each ankle is tied separately, whether spreadeagle or with the lower limbs closer together. For some people, gagging adds some florid grace notes—but be extremely careful not to block breathing, or use anything that's going to hurt (like adhesive tape, removing which can rip your lips off) or be so thorough as to prevent some signaling if anything goes wrong.

Once your lover is secured, you make love to her as you might otherwise or, better yet, you do things that both of you have discussed in advance. This pre-lovemaking conference can add to your mutual enjoyment by stimulating fantasies of what it will be like when you really do it. Indeed, the sharing of sexual fantasies is part and parcel of pleasurable lovemaking and can enhance your repertoire by legitimizing acts—such as bondage—that you might otherwise be too shy or afraid to try.

It is probably unnecessary in a book for women who like to make love with women to stress the importance of avoiding cruelty, violence or injury. Bondage should be a game of love, not of spite. If you're angry with your partner, talk it out. *Don't* act it out by engaging in thinly disguised torture or by getting too much into the role of "dominating" someone who is helplessly tied.

Boots If your patent leather mary jane slippers once announced to the world that you were a proper little girl, your style in boots these days declares not only that you're a proper lesbian but that you're a particular kind of proper lesbian.

A lesbian in boots that are thick leather, heavy-heeled, vaguely cowboy-ish is a lesbian announcing that she is freewheeling, sexually assertive, prepared to make a lot of noise and willing to try just about anything. Especially when she wears tight jeans as well, this lesbian is presenting an image of herself she means you to understand as purely sexual: as she is turned on by wearing these boots, she means you to be turned on by watching her move in them. Boots of a lesser sexual order—soft soled, high-heeled or with pointed toes—convey a lady-like image which, sexually, connotes an unstylish passivity and timidity. Heavy boots are not restricted to butches. They are usually not worn these days to signify sexual roles but to show liberation from the restriction of roles. Boot-wearing, however, typically ends at the bedroom door: on the feet, up to the knees, they are erotic foreplay; in bed, they mean little more than torn sheets.

Breakfast in bed A leisurely, luxurious breakfast in bed on a morning neither of you has to go to work can be a delightful prelude or follow-up to lovemaking or stand by itself as shared sensuality of the most deliciously indulgent variety.

It's best to alternate who does the preparing and serving or one of you may end up feeling like kitchen help. Be sure the bed is well equipped with pillows to lounge against and to support serving trays so that things don't slosh about when you pause to kiss or caress.

For really special occasions, champagne and orange juice (half and half) or a bloody mary will be good for starters. If you don't want alcohol, try mixing club soda with orange juice or making a virgin mary (Tabasco sauce, Worcester, seasoning and lemon juice). Plain orange or tomato juice are fine, but less festive.

Try locking arms Tyrolean style and drinking from each other's glass. Try holding a modest amount in your mouth so your lover can suck it into her own as you kiss. Try putting tiny drops on her nipples and then licking it off. Try talking dirty into your glass as you peek over its rim to watch her reactions. And, by all means, trade off.

Inject some sexuality into what is already a highly sensual scene.

The main course should be elaborate in the sense of being special or non-workday, but simple to prepare. This is a moment to savor, not for rushing from the bed to turn over something in a frying pan. Fried eggs on frozen waffles are very quick to do, but cold food is even easier. It's all a matter of what the two of you want.

When you return to bed with the serving trays it is time not only for leisurely eating but for more pecking, nibbling, kisses, fondling and, eventually, what have you. By all means, feed each other. Pop little morsels of food into each other's mouths, or pass your lover's coffee cup not into her hands but directly against her lips.

Breasts Breasts are exquisitely erogenous zones, and who but another woman should know better how much a woman likes to have them fondled, manipulated, kissed and sucked? Who but another woman can know the pleasure of a close embrace—breast to breast?

A natural is attending to one breast by mouth and the other by hand, alternating as you proceed. Sometimes it is nice to concentrate on all but the nipple—saving it for dessert or, put another way, as a first course before the entrée of genital contact. You can stroke (feathery light, then heavier) knead, run the fingernails against and generally fondle the whole area. You can trace from the armpit down around the bottom of the breast, then up along the breastbone and out along the clavicle. With the palm of the hand directly centered over the nipple, gently squeeze the whole breast in an in-and-out motion, using the thumb and each finger to play keyboard exercises against the flesh they contact. The nipple itself can be flicked, encircled, gently pulled, then you can focus on the motion or combination of motions she seems most to enjoy.

Mouth contact will probably evoke the more excited response. Again, don't target the nipple for immediate attention (unless, in her already excited state, she indicates that's what she wants). The mouth should not neglect the same lines and curves the hand is tracing; bathe each section in broad tongue-washes and kisses of varying intensity. Approach the nipple with the tongue tip, working round and round it before kissing. You can suck and pull gently (harder if she desires); lick both with the tip of the tongue and with its full breadth. Don't be afraid to make lots of noise, as many women are further excited by the sound of sucking and lapping.

Simultaneous stimulation is easily achieved if that's what both of you want (some lesbians prefer to trade off, finding the whole experience too stimulating to attend to more than one enjoyment at a time). If your lover is lying flat on her back, you can approach from the side at a slight diagonal. The knee closest to her head is placed

by her shoulder, with most of your torso aimed footward. The other knee is somewhere near the middle of her arm. As you lean over her to kiss and suck the breast and nipple on the side farthest from where you are kneeling, your own breast falls to her mouth.

There are many variations—for example, kneeling directly above her head and simply leaning downward—and anatomical differences will dictate the position which is most comfortable and satisfying.

Many lesbians like to continue breast play during genital love-making and some, through tightening muscles and thigh-squeezing (described under *Tribadism*), come without the "active" partner's attention below the breastline.

Bush Pubic hair is a sexual plaything as eloquent with pleasure as you make it. If you imagine it as a little forest guarding entry to the pleasure dome it surrounds it can take on the richness of fantasy, and when that happens the bush begins to get the attention it deserves. You can twirl it in your fingers, brush your face against it, use a soft brush on it, stroke it, pull it. Decorate it with a little bow and then go down on her. If you can endure the discomfort of bristles, use a safety razor and shape the top of it into the twin curves of a heart for a unique valentine surprise.

Butch/femme   Back in the days when role-playing in the style of straight couples was more common, butch referred to the "masculine" partner, femme to the "feminine" in a lesbian relationship. Both roles were adopted and acted out with dead seriousness, with very little deviation. Although much butch/femme role-playing stopped at the bedroom door (where butches could suddenly become very "feminine" and vice versa), in other aspects of the couple's lives the entire personality and temperament were pervaded with the behavior assumed to be appropriate to the role (see *Role-playing*). Pathetically, this behavior was generally a parody of the worst heterosexual coupling: the butch stomping and hen-pecked, the femme kittenish and nagging. The straight double-standard in sexual activity also operated among such couples, the butch feeling compelled (whether she wanted to or not) to act like a tomcat, and the femme constrained to the purely monogamous attachment.

Unfortunately, generations of lesbians were brain-washed into believing that one role or the other came "naturally" to them, and that being "kiki" (neither butch nor femme: just lesbian) was to be contemptibly wishy-washy or at best uninitiated. In extreme cases the psychological damage to the butch partner consisted of an outright denial of her womanhood and surrender of control over her sexual life. In some instances the butch would refuse to undress for bed, at least from the waist up: the sight of breasts would blow the masculine image for the femme and weaken the necessary self-image for the butch. Further, the butch was always "on top" and, at the expense of her own orgasm, refused to let the femme touch her. The fantasy was more critical to the butch than sexual pleasure.

The situation for most femmes, however, was more ambivalent: they could, under the proper circumstances (becoming attracted to someone even "femmier" than themselves was one) slip into the butch role; or, with another kind of woman, abandon roles altogether and become kiki. The femme could even (as a lot of old lesbian porn and pulp romances indicate) as easily go with a man and continue to play the passive, submissive role in bed and out, but this happened rarely. Although female conditioning and even physical attributes— she might have been too petite, too conventionally pretty to adopt the butch swagger—led her to respond to a masculine image, the femme was still thoroughly lesbian: she needed ultimately the sexual reality of a woman.

We write as if this situation is all in the past—and for the most part it is. With heightened awareness of sexual possibilities and variety, fewer people are entertained for very long by role-playing. Also current social analysis has helped bring a greater understanding that a woman does not have to be a "man" to love a woman.

Buttocks In the erotic hierarchy they are usually second only to breasts in their capacity for suggestiveness and stimulation. In visual terms, however, different lesbians mean different things when they think of "a good ass." Narrow, almost boyish buttocks—especially when they're encased in tight pants which exaggerate every shift and sway of the flesh—are the fashionable favorite, but what catches the eye on the street is not necessarily what catches the breath in bed.

No matter what the shape, buttocks are the most malleable portions of the human body, just asking to be squeezed, spanked, pummelled, massaged, stroked, licked. A special sexual treat among lesbians is the "buttock kiss" in which one lies on top of the other, buttocks to buttocks, and both engage in deep rhythmic pressure and response—the one on the bottom pressing up, the one on top pushing down. An activity with much higher orgasmic potential, however, involves one partner mounting one of her lover's buttocks and moving up and down, backward and forward until she comes. In this, your right (or left) knee is supporting you between her legs (and your knees can be giving her clitoral stimulation too in this position) while your other knee is against her waist. If you are rubbing on her left buttock, you can also employ your right hand and fingers in her crotch, using your right knee against your hand for added pressure. Mutual orgasm is very possible in this position.

Celibacy Whimsically enough, the dictionary definition of "celibacy" is "the state of being unmarried." Thus lesbians who live together are celibate!

But, if one equates celibacy with abstinence, then there are certainly times at which an individual may choose to abstain. But we feel this is definitely an individual choice, and therefore would not presume to enumerate examples of what we as individuals may judge to be sound reasons. We would, however, suggest serious questioning and reconsideration of any strictures imposed by societal, religious or intrapsychic canons against lesbian lovemaking. We would further question any abstinence that includes not masturbating: all people have both a biological and psychological need for sexual release, and the need should not be allowed to wither away from inactivity and, most likely, contribute to other biological and psychological witherings.

Cheeks A compliment paid to your facial cheeks may well be meant to flatter the cheeks on the other side of your body. "Cheeky": insolent, cooly confident, showing effrontery; "cheek-by-jowl": side by side in the closest intimacy; "dancing cheek-to-cheek" is open to interpretation.

Children of lesbians Lesbians have always existed. Therefore children of lesbians have always existed.

We think, though, that today's children of lesbians are better loved, more loving, healthier and better adjusted than in any era to date. The reasons are simple. Up until the present century most lesbians who bore children stayed within the heterosexual family framework. They had little choice, given the economic structure. This is pretty much what many straight women did too, often despising their mate, resenting their own lack of fulfillment, being sick and tired of pregnancy, housework, the limitations of a social life centered on sewing bees and church suppers, envying their girl children's sense of freedom and worrying about the day that it, too, would pass. But added to this was the lesbian's essential preference for loving another woman, as well as, in most instances, heightened resentment at the insurmountable obstacles to the realization of her own ambitiousness, her own individuality. Children from such a background tended to grow up cool, cautious and distant, always afraid of something they could sense, but which was never discussed.

This pattern was broken in the earlier decades of this century—but often only in comfortable, upper-class settings (especially in England), where it was, at least relatively and with discretion, O.K. to be gay and hence O.K. to be warm, loving, giving, and receptive with your lover. Children were free to respond accordingly.

It took a while for this attitude to cross class lines and the ocean. But there is now a sizable number of adults who were raised by lesbian couples, single lesbians—sometimes with and sometimes without a partner—lesbians married to gay men (both acknowledging their homosexuality, and open about gay affairs) or by lesbians who came out late and left the straight world, taking their children with them.

These adults (at least all the ones we know of) are truly beautiful people. Maybe because they were freed from the Blessed Product myth (see *Lesbian motherhood*); maybe because, more than other children, they grew up in an atmosphere of tolerance and acceptance; maybe because they understood quite early on that they could be themselves—not an extension of daddy (or mommy); maybe because they were not lied to. For example, "I never felt any of that guilt the kids of divorced parents often feel. I knew I hadn't done anything wrong. I even knew that my father wasn't some sort of beast, but that he just happened to be a man and mom preferred women." Alternatively: "Mother always told me the truth about what she felt or thought, but she never tried to force me to agree. For her, lesbianism was the preferred life-style. Well, I happen to be straight—but I think my life's a helluva lot richer for knowing and loving people who aren't."

But what about some of the problems children of lesbians can have? The little girl faced by a bigger boy who calls her mother a '"dirty queer" typifies the dilemma. She is brought up in an atmosphere of love, caring, lack of bigotry, and with the support system offered by the large network of interesting friends who comprise a special kind of extended family. She knows that there is nothing dirty about mother or queer about her homosexuality, but she will need guidance. Substitute any number of nouns for "queer"—dirty Nigger, dirty Wop, dirty Jew, dirty any word—and you can appreciate the lesbian's position as she tries to help her child.

In later childhood or early adolescence when differences often seem so threatening, children of lesbians may wish their family were more standard. One approach is to collaborate on a list of all the things you both like and enjoy about your family; sometimes sharpening the differences can help to level the value judgments of good and bad.

A surprising number of children of lesbians experience a sense of crisis and trauma when, in their late teens or early twenties, they become aware of their own sexuality and discover they are straight. Surprising because we know, personally or clinically, of no lesbian to whom the matter has been of great concern. Again, lesbians tend to treat their children as people with their own individual personalities, not as extensions of themselves. On the other hand, the situation is not surprising from the child's standpoint. Most lesbians who have children are good mothers, and children have a natural tendency to want to emulate such parents. However, lest this cause the straight world undue concern about the proliferation of gay people, let us hastily point out that there is *no* evidence indicating that proportionately more gay people emerge from gay homes. To think otherwise is to accept an error very much like believing that straight people who have gay children are "failures" as parents.

Should such an "I'm-straight" crisis occur with your child, talk it over honestly. If you agree that outside intervention might be helpful, seek a mental health professional who is sympathetic to the problem and experienced in dealing with it.

The flip side of the situation can occur if your child does choose homosexuality. On the one hand, it should not matter. On the other hand, especially for lesbians who have not managed completely to break from societal expectations they were raised with, you, too, might wonder if you've been a failure as a parent. Close, sincere, mutually introspective discussion with your child, with or without a counselor, should do the trick.

Finally, one should always bear in mind that the children of lesbians learn like the children of any people. They are nurtured on adults' behavior toward them, and on the behavior between adults who share their young lives. If both by direct experience and observation they learn about loving, caring and living a meaningful life, the sexual orientation of their models will be of supreme unconcern.

Civil rights Because of the lesbian's peculiar invisibility in homosexual history, her civil liberties have been, and still are, more inextricably united with the cause of women in general than with the gay rights movements. When attacks on gays are made, the image bigots have in mind is typically male, stereotypically "faggot." Only incidentally, and as a second thought, do the "dykes" come to mind. The "loss" of a male to homosexuality is regarded as a waste of heterosexual power and privilege and of male bonding in particular. Those men (and their women) who persecute homosexual males hate and fear, more than any other thing, women and "the feminine." Their rage against "faggots" is directed against the femininity they imagine to be intrinsic to the homosexual character. Those who attempt to deny homosexuals jobs and housing also are opposed to abortion, lesbian motherhood, equal pay for equal work, a woman (a Black or a Jew) in the White House, and freedom of any religious, political or sexual choice.

Recognition of misogyny as the root cause of the hysteria directed against homosexuals causes considerable feelings of ambivalence. While lesbians, for the most part, have a sense of kinship with the outcast status of the gay male, they are at the same time painfully aware of the simple male–female pattern of injustices that also exist: when a gay "passes" he passes as a man, with all the power accorded to straight men. When a lesbian passes, she passes as a woman—with all the powerlessness women are heir to. When lesbians make common cause it is with those minorities who recognize this fact of life. The politically wise lesbian (she who wishes survival for herself as well as for others) makes lesbian/women's needs a non-negotiable priority before joining up. Since women, traditionally, have not been imaged as sexually active beings (at least, not "good" women) they have also been regarded as less sexually menacing than men. Thus, most of the barrage against gays has concentrated on men and the barrage against women has fallen on lesbians, since they are considered to be the most sexually active (therefore the most menacing) of females. Fear of women and fear of sexuality is, therefore, the basis of legal discrimination and social and economic strictures against gay people. In the fight for civil rights, lesbians who understand the "double jeopardy" of being both female and gay have also understood that the freedom of women—as well as the freedom of gays—is of the essence. Politically experienced people have learned that gay liberation is ultimately inseparable from women's liberation.

Cleanliness Whether fantasy or not, there is a belief abroad that women are more naturally fastidious about cleanliness than men are. Perhaps, then, there is little need to stress the importance of personal hygiene in a book directed to lesbians, except that there are pockets of confusion about the anatomy of sex and therefore there may be some mystery about exactly what needs to be cleaned.

For example, just as uncircumcised men can have some difficulties with what is rather onomatopoeiacally called smegma, women can accumulate what *Dorland's Illustrated Medical Dictionary* calls this "thick, cheesy, ill-smelling secretion" around their clitoris. It's nothing to worry about, being no more than sloughed-off natural material, but proper removal requires careful and gentle washing with the clitoral sheath pulled closer toward the front of your body. (Use a mirror unless you are unusually athletic.)

Occasional vaginal douching may be in order, particularly after menstruation or copious discharge related to sex, not infection. (In the latter case, don't tarry about consulting a gynecologist—both for your sake and your lover's.) Although you may understandably object on political grounds to swelling the profits of companies who manufacture the plethora of "feminine hygiene" products, the packaged preparations are often better suited to maintaining the vagina's natural acid balance than home-made solutions.

Going from front to rear, so to speak—which is also the direction toilet paper should go—take special care to wash both the perineum and anal area with vigor. The transmission of bacteria toward the vagina and vaginal products to the clitoral area is to be avoided.

Of course, cleanliness is by no means confined to the crotch. The whole body is the object of lovemaking, and nothing is quite so off-putting as the bad smell and acrid taste of unwashed skin. The same goes for hair—which is, in dancing or an initial embrace—often the first part of you that reaches a potential lover's nose. Some women who would never consider omitting a daily shower or bath are wont to wait ten days or two weeks to wash their hair. Don't.

Finally, bathing together makes for wonderful sharing. Keeping clean should never be a chore.

Clit lit At last we have a worthwhile, non-pornographic lesbian literature—fiction, poetry and essays written by lesbians, about lesbians and, most importantly, from a completely lesbian point of view. Fifteen years ago it would have consisted largely of Radclyffe Hall's *The Well of Loneliness*, Rosamund Lehmann's *Dusty Answer* and "drugstore paperbacks" the theme of which was almost always the same: femme meets butch (usually in Greenwich Village); drunkenness, violence and heavy (but very unspecified) sex ensue; femme ponders the problems of being "different" and outcast; the young man in the background quickly replaces the butch in the foreground and we close on a vision of a heterosexual cottage covered with heterosexual ivy. The butch either commits suicide straight off, begins to drink herself to death or finds a new "innocent" to corrupt.

Five years ago it would have been possible to list on half a page titles and publishers answering such silly self-destructiveness with the truth about lesbian reality—that is, that lesbians are human as well as sexual beings, with rich and interesting lives beyond the bedroom and the bar. Today, however, such titles, presses and publishers have proliferated to such a marvelous extent that it would take a hundred pages to list them all. We feel that some outline of their availability, however, is still essential because we know that sexual isolation and its accompanying neuroses diminish in direct proportion to one's sense of belonging, of having a cultural identity.

Film and television are still often timid and/or hostile in their portrayal of lesbians, still relying by and large on stereotypes of social and psychological evil to give their audiences the thrill of the "big bad dyke": at best, an ugly bitch, at worst, a murderer. It's no surprise that lesbians (whether publishers know it or not) form the largest percentage of the book-buying public. It's still, however, a problem for lesbians outside urban areas to know where and what to find of positive literature about themselves, which is why we have included a select bibliography at the end of the book.

Clitoris The clitoris is the center of every woman's sexual universe. Unless the clitoris is stimulated, all the sweet nothings whispered in her ear and all the pumping into her vagina will not produce orgasm in a woman.

Women have recently given some serious thought to the metaphysical implications of the clitoris: since it is the only part of the human anatomy, male or female, that serves no other function than to produce sexual pleasure and orgasm, is it possible that women have reached sexual perfection on the evolutionary scale? Is it possible that all religious, medical and psychoanalytic dogma aimed at persuading woman that her natural and sacred purpose on earth is to give sexual pleasure to man and produce his [sic] children is one grand conspiracy to keep the clitoris out of sight, mind and touch? However these questions resolve themselves in the relative sexual freedom (or lack of it) for women in general, it is sensible to assume that much of the societally-induced guilt and shame that has been dumped on lesbians has come about because lesbians, like the clitoris, participate in sex for no other reason that the sheer fun of it all.

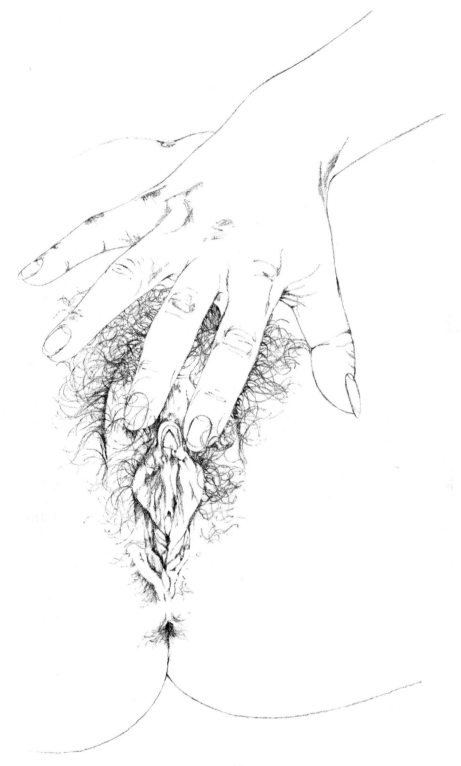

Usually, when consideration is given to the clitoris at all, it is referred to as an analogue to the penis—yet one more instance when the male body is used as the standard for yet another erroneous comparison: the production of orgasm, in fact, is the only function that the clitoris and the penis share. When not engaged sexually, the penis is used for urination; when stimulated, it becomes erect; in orgasm, it ejaculates semen. The clitoris, when not fulfilling its single glorious destiny, simply lies in wait, tucked in its labial nest waiting on its owner's erotic will. An even odder misconception about the clitoris comes about through clitoris/penis association: the presumption that the lesbian "personality" (as if there were only one) is masculine in character; that the lesbian thinks "like a man," behaves sexually as if she were a man and—most ludicrous of all—pretends she's a man when she makes love. In fact if there is such a thing as an utterly clitoral (i.e. lesbian) personality based on sexual function it would be the exact opposite of the penile (male) sexual "personality." Male orgasm consists of a thrust/spurt/explosion. Female orgasm is a phenomenon of radiating circles lapping in shuddering waves from the eye of the storm. If people feel compelled to generalize about personality from anatomical particulars, they would do well to keep this circular effect in mind.

Perhaps the truest index to the patriarchal attitudes toward clitoral rapture has been the gruesome practice of clitorectomy—a surgical procedure that by removing the hood of the clitoris permanently divests the organ of all sensation. *The Joy of Sex* declares clitorectomy the practice of "benighted savages." Unfortunately, it has also been known to happen in such "civilized" nations as the United States.

Closets   Coming out means acknowledging your gayness. Coming out of the closet means letting it be known that you are gay.

We don't mean climbing onto rooftops *à la* King Kong, beating your breast and proclaiming to the world in general: "Look here, I'm *gay!*" or, unless you are motivated to test public tolerance and perhaps to effect change, passionately to kiss your lover while seated in a restaurant that will probably toss you out.

We do, however, mean letting all the people significant in your life—family, friends, co-workers, employers, employees—know where you stand. Not from self-assertion or arrogance, or in any "testing-the-limits" sense, but simply because *the air inside closets is stifling*. The energy of pretending to be something other than what you are is too draining; it depletes you physically and often has the psychological effect of backfiring so that you may begin to believe that "they" are right and there is something wrong about you.

Fortunately, the public's increased awareness of the fact of every-body's essential bisexuality, plus the strides made by Women's Liberation and Gay Lib, have fostered a climate of more acceptance. Still, all is not roses for the lesbian who wants to come out of the closet but feels—often with indisputable justification—that she is jeopardizing her career if she does. Too, some lesbians believe (again, with indisputable justification) that they can better serve the "cause" (for example, in supporting the admission of open lesbians into their work setting) if they are not yet themselves generally known to be gay.

Whatever your own position on this question, your lover's must be taken into consideration if you want to maintain and further build a solid relationship. If you are out and she is not, try to under-stand and respect her reasons. If she is out and you are not, seek that understanding and respect from her. You are both free to explore, re-examine and perhaps modify your own positions. But don't try to force agreement and above all don't try to make your lover feel guilty or inadequate because of her stance. A lot of tender, caring and mutually respecting negotiations will be in order to determine where, when and under what circumstances you are both totally open, and where, when and under what circumstances you must both be circumspect in order to preserve the relationship itself (assuming that it is your first priority).

Perhaps, at least at first, some compromise may be in order. Maybe both families can know (an amazing number of lesbians cling to the outdated notion that a never-darken-my-door-again attitude will be assumed, when rarely is this the case), as can all your straight friends (again, experiment with telling; most people love you more when you trust them to share "secrets"). This degree of coming out of the closet is often enough to relieve the tension a couple may be experiencing, as well as enabling you to breathe more easily. It can also be good preparation for a total coming out, if that becomes possible (see also *Coming out*).

Clothes Clothes may indeed "make the man" in terms of image and identity. But clothes do not, as it is popularly supposed, make the lesbian. It is impossible to identify a lesbian by what she's got on her back, so don't go around these days hunting for silk neck-ties and pin-stripe suits in hopes of finding the reincarnation of Radclyffe Hall. Lesbians wear pink chiffon and lesbians wear black leather jackets. Lesbians wear bikinis and lesbians wear tank suits. Lesbians wear everything clothes manu-facturers put on the market, whether it's designed for men or for women. Role associations with clothes have practically vanished except in play (see also *Drag* and *Little theater*).

Coming out   Coming out as a lesbian is nothing more, and nothing less, than acknowledging your own gayness. Coming out is also the first step you take in growing into the glued-together, giving-and-taking individual you want to be— an individual whose sexual preference is as much a part of her personality, her taste and temperament as having brown hair or enjoying classical guitar.

It should be understood that as lesbians see it nothing is more natural than a woman loving another woman, someone who feels like you, is built like you, tends to think and react as you do.

If that still sounds unnatural to you, consider for a moment a poster written and drawn by Alan Wakeman (published in 1975 by the Gay Sweatshop). Sporting lots of captioned arrows moving in and out of a circle, the poster is titled: "What Exactly Is Heterosexuality and What Causes It?" The text explains that some heterosexuals claim they've always been that way (they were born like that), some blame an early experience with someone of the opposite sex, some agree with authorities who point to hormonal imbalances and no one is quite sure how to cure it.

At least one point in traditional psychologic/psychiatric thinking is agreeably correct and underscores what we all know to be true from experience: a child's first love is a woman—mother or mother surrogate. The problems little boys may experience with this situation have been amply documented, in imaginative as well as in psychoanalytic literature. But no matter how bad it gets for them, they have a clear advantage over little girls: they have, at least, started out loving the "right" sex. Little girls, on the other hand, barely have the time to consider woman-loving before they are rushed headlong into training meant to make them respond instead to people entirely different: hairy, hard-bodied, deep-voiced, massive. And who, by common agreement in many cultures, are and have been regarded (witness the record of the visual arts) as aesthetically inferior. Little girls, in effect, learn quite early on that they must love and pursue that which much of the world regards as second-best.

What seems remarkable to lesbians is not that so many females choose to go gay, but that so many get straight and stay straight. But the changes are happening—the fact that this book exists and you are reading it is only one indication that this is so. Lesbians are moving out of the bars, into the streets, into your neighborhood. The straight world is waking (sometimes painfully) to the fact that the "monster" is a human being who not only makes love but who also works, spends money, sometimes raises children, who wishes for a place in the country or at the ocean. And it's being recorded that while lesbians sometimes fight, and sometimes split, they are producing better track records at maintaining relationships than straight couples. We think this may reflect lesbians' enormous practice in the art of negotiation, but more of that later.

Are there more lesbians today than ever there were before? It's popular to think so and either blame or praise the more relaxed social climate for making this the case—as if the "liberated" society were a factory assembly-line bringing lesbians to you at popular prices. The fact is that there were always lesbians, but they married men, or joined a convent, or became the best teacher you ever had or were your "spinster" aunts. Gay and Women's Liberation have not manufactured lesbians. These movements have simply made it easier to be a lesbian if that's what you really are.

Previously, a common folk-remedy for being a girl was to "kiss your elbow" and turn into a boy. Your attempt, and failure at, this impossible task was meant not only to teach you that you couldn't have mother (only boys can love women), but that you'd never have any of the other things you noticed boys and men enjoying: power, status, interesting occupations, more physical freedom, as well as the love and admiration of women. Our thesis, backed by a great deal of personal investigation as well as clinical data, is that the single prime motivation for young girls becoming tomboys (or moody intellectuals) has been that being "male" allows you to love women and be loved in return.

But hardly one of these tree-climbing Tarzanas or compulsive readers got to keep on doing what came naturally: loving what the world declared it was best to love. Sooner or later most of them gritted their teeth and forced themselves into bras and girdles and crinoline petticoats and went out there and pretended to be "women". Many, too, compounded this abnormal (for them) condition by marrying or having straight affairs. Though they knew somehow that what was "normal" wasn't necessarily healthy for them, proving that knowledge and living by it was another matter. Columbus knew the world wasn't flat, but it took him three ships, a queen's ransom and a trip around the earth to show them he was right. For the thoroughly repressed woman-loving woman the knowledge consisted of surges in the pit of the stomach when she ran into the dark-eyed sorority sister down the hall. Knowledge was enduring Harold's French kisses but being thrilled by the English teacher in the tailored suit.

Then, suddenly (for the lucky ones), this knowledge was documented and you weren't any longer the only lesbian in the world. You discovered *The Well of Loneliness* and, despite the novel's miserable attitudes on sin, guilt and "inversion," a lesbian had written it. Typically, too, a gay man discovered you, got you to talk about it and showed you the "city" hiding behind the big city; even more important, he often had a social entrée to a circle of lesbians.

Or, it was as simple a matter as reaching out and touching her hand one night at the movies.

The gist of all this discovery (and this still holds true) was that contrary to everything you'd been taught the world was simply filled with women who love women—and not as fake men, but as women. The aloneness went, so did sexual frustration and so did feeling like a freak.

But society was another story: you learned you could still be treated like a freak by your boss, your neighbors, your parents. One professional woman, now in her mid-forties, says "Back in the '50s I used to be asked; 'Do you lead a double life?' I always answered, 'No, triple.' There was me the college professor who always acted straight; me the dutiful daughter who figured my family must know—but we'd best not talk about it; and me the lesbian who was in love with a woman."

Until relatively recently, all these pieces fitted together to make a picture of your fairly typical lesbian, many of them highly successful in business or the professions, valued as outstanding employees wherever they worked, but so afraid to come out of the closet (and for good reason) that they drained off a lot of energy every day in elaborate cover-ups—cover-ups ranging from the most absurdly feminine dress styles to chatter about the "boyfriend" (who was usually a gay man equally in need of a heterosexual mask).

Today there are fewer cover-ups, not more lesbians than previously. And if lesbians these days seem to be getting younger, it simply means that the so-called sexual revolution, with its air of increased permissiveness, has generated a more open expression of love's possibilities. The young lesbian these days will more frequently bring her college roommate home for Christmas holidays rather than run for a temporary hideout in the city's bars.

Bars however were not the only answer for lesbians of the older generation. In 1939 or 1949, for example, when inseparable-friend housewives used to rush their children off to school in order to share some time over coffee, they may have been sublimating love into recipe-sharing. A hundred years ago, many of the women stitching quilts and canning pears together were doing the same; and today, still, so are a good proportion of those housewives who live for their Thursday night out with the Ladies' Bowling Team.

What we are experiencing today, therefore, is more manifest female homosexuality than formerly. For that, thank the Goddesses, who came to earth in the form of T-shirted young women with the guts to bust up a male monopoly on defining what's right and wrong and what's well and sick. But the most cursory dip into your grandmother's old diary (not to mention some great literature dating

back to Sappho) should alone be enough to persuade anyone that, far from being an "aberration of nature," women loving women has been with us since the beginning—almost as if nature herself had planned it that way.

But does love always imply sexuality? We have the great Freud himself to thank for believing that it probably does. So the question then becomes: Does a person always have to act on love's underlying sexuality?

Of course not. People not only feel, they also think. They feel attractions and think what to do about them, and because lesbians have always had to think ahead and think hard to survive, let alone flourish, they are perhaps better at letting thought guide their feelings than many straight women, who have a simpler set of rules to live by.

The point is to know not only your gut feelings but also what your life is: your mores and morals, your goals, your style; your deeply personal values and expectations.

Once this concept of the integrated person is grasped, one is truly free to be a lesbian. Heterosexuals by and large don't know that they are "straight" and resent and resist being defined by what they do in bed. Lesbians should give themselves (even if no one else does) the same freedom of definition. You are already a daughter. You may be or may want to be a mother. You are a worker, a professional, an artist, a thinker, a dreamer, a lover. Chances are you're somebody's sister, cousin, niece or aunt. You may be a Presbyterian, a Catholic or an agnostic; a Democrat, a Republican or a member of the National Organization for Women. Would you define yourself—your complete self—by any one of these descriptions?

The gender of whom one loves does not create the problem *per se*. Almost never do lesbians seek (or need) psychotherapeutic help because they are lesbians: sexual orientation on its own brings few people to shrinks, and mental health professionals—unless they are too biased or ignorant to recognize it—soon discover this fact. People complain of many things, but seldom of the gender of whom they are attracted to, unless they have been purposefully and cruelly brainwashed into this attitude. All things being equal, it is problems like work, money, jealousy, lack of response, infidelity, intimacy-versus-space conflicts, incompatibility or a terrible childhood that won't let go that make people suffer.

Do these problems sound peculiar to homosexuals, female or male, or does the problem lie elsewhere? The courts currently grant divorces to at least one-third of all heterosexuals who marry other heterosexuals.

So we return to our initial point. Coming out is nothing more, but nothing less, than acknowledging your own gayness as part of your total self: the reality that makes you who you are; your life that is a process of growing into your total being. And that's essentially what this book is about. If you are a lesbian, your life—sexual, social, intellectual, emotional—need not suffer, but can flourish, be rich and rewarding (see also *Closets*).

Consciousness raising Consciousness raising has, historically, been the keystone of all impulses, organized or not, toward liberation of minority groups. In the mid-1960s the first consciousness raising groups were organized by women to explore the effects of growing up female in a male-dominated society. These groups proliferated to such an extent, and so quickly, that today there is hardly a corner of the country left in which weekly meetings do not occur—in private homes and apartments, local women's centers, even sometimes spontaneously on street corners and bar stools.

Typically, the first goal of a C.R. group is to discover what the members of the group have in common as women, despite discrepancies in class, race or ethnic background and in present economic, political and social differences. The establishment, early on, of a sense of shared oppression, and a shared desire to end that oppression, goes a long way in creating an almost palpable sense of bonding within the group. Such bonding becomes especially critical to the group's future when (again, typically) the individual members begin to explore how women as well as men oppress other women through privilege that has been either inherited (skin color, education, social background, etc.) or earned ("I worked hard and pulled myself up by my own bootstraps. Why can't you?"). Frequently, the group rides out the emotional and often traumatizing storm that revelation of difference incites, but only if the group constantly reminds itself that no matter what the differences and no matter how embittering those differences can be the situation that brought the group together is still there: that women belong to the world's oldest minority group.

Sooner or later, however, the issue of sexual preference will arise and it is on the issue of sex that C.R. groups may either rise or fall, continue to meet or to reorganize into particularized segments. Often, reorganization is a necessity. The straight members have reached the point where they feel it is urgent to discuss strictly heterosexual matters such as rape within marriage, abortion, heterosexual privilege, enlightening or divorcing husbands, sexual difficulties with men. Lesbians, who were either out of the closet before the group, or who came out as a result of the group's encouragement and support, need to discuss specifically lesbian issues, such as coming out to parents and/or children, coming out on the job, internalized effects of oppression that manifest themselves in role-playing, self-contempt, difficulties in relationships.

These days lesbians tend to skip the mixed groups and form or join all-lesbian groups at the outset. In our experience, the disadvantages of omitting the mixed-group stage far outweigh the advantages. While inevitable gay–straight conflicts are avoided, the learning process inherent within the conflict in a sincerely committed mixed group is also missed. More critically, the political support that gay women need from straight women is never created. Frequently, it is only in mixed C.R. groups that heterosexual women learn at a gut level that *no* woman can be free until *all* women are free. Lesbians, too (often to their surprise), realize that no lesbian is free until all women are free.

Consciousness raising formats vary according to the nature of the group. At one extreme, some exist simply as support groups to help their members survive day-to-day pressures and to ameliorate personal problems. Others are solely and often militantly political in organization and goals. Classic C.R. groups, however, seek to relate the personal to the political, to seek an end to individual pain in political change. One of the fundamental principles of consciousness raising is that there is no such thing as the "individual solution" to oppression. The euphoria of finding a new lover, for example, may for a while make all problems seem inconsequential, but the group's purpose is to remind each other that personal happiness must not be used as a retreat from serious commitment, that a better orgasm or a better job does not call a halt to rape or wife beating or harassment of lesbians once they're out of their bedrooms and on the job or in the streets. It is in this respect that consciousness raising most profoundly differs from group therapy: personal problems find their solution only when they are dealt with in the context of political awareness; that personal change can only, finally, be found and given complete expression in political change. Almost all women experience one thing in common in the consciousness raising experience—that a particular shame, sorrow, terror or fantasy they believed uniquely their own is also shared by other women, thus liberating the individual woman from a sense of isolation or self-hate.

Both personal and political changes can be effected by following these guidelines:

1. No more than ten members to a group unless you are able to devote from two to three hours to each weekly session.
2. Once you have joined the group you must give it utmost priority. The group will not be effective for you or for the other members if you attend only when you feel like it.

3. The group is leaderless. "Natural" leaders—those who tend to dominate situations either verbally or through their personalities—must suppress the urge to do so. When they don't, the other members must let them know what they're doing.

4. Do not confuse the group with a social event. Don't serve or expect alcohol or drugs to ease the situation. Start on time.

5. Each member must be given an allotted uninterrupted time to speak. Once she has used up her time, she must be silent. Equal speaking time is essential to maintaining the group's balance of power.

6. Practice acceptance. Don't ridicule or invalidate another woman's experience by expressing shock or disbelief at what she says. Response must be positive; otherwise, be silent.

7. Do not attempt to "instruct" the other group members. You are there to match your experiences with those of others, and not to impress or to educate.

8. Use the first meeting to introduce yourself in terms of your background, your sexual experiences, your ambitions, your present "place" in life. If you have a political position, state that too.

9. Before each meeting ends, select the topic for the next meeting and stick to it. Groups of long standing often reserve some time for personal emergencies and occasionally might cancel the evening's topic to devote the full time to a solution. If "emergencies" begin to happen all the time to certain individuals, then the group should put its collective foot down. The group does not exist to act as either therapist or mother to women who covet attention.

10. Speak from the heart. Do not objectify either your own or others' experience. In the group process, a stage will naturally be reached when it is time to abandon the personal testimony and begin to abstract and analyze personal experience in terms of society. The third stage is reached when the group is ready to organize itself into some form of action.

11. Do not become romantically or sexually involved with another group member while the group still exists. If this can't be avoided, one or both of the new lovers should leave the group and join or form new ones separately.

12. Absolute confidentiality must be observed to maintain trust.

Women who have gone through the consciousness raising experience generally believe it to be one of the most enlightening events of their lives. The process provides a kind of self-knowledge and a knowledge of the external world that cannot be learned in any other place. A "sister" found in C.R. is a sister for ever.

Do not, however, become discouraged when your group comes to an end or avoid ending the group when you begin to repeat yourselves.

Crème de la crème   The sexual "cream" that the vagina spills during orgasm; what you drink from your "demitasse." A lesbian who's rapturously spoken of as "crème de la crème" simply couldn't be better both in bed and out; a rare creature every lesbian in love thinks she's captured and every lesbian out of love is waiting for.

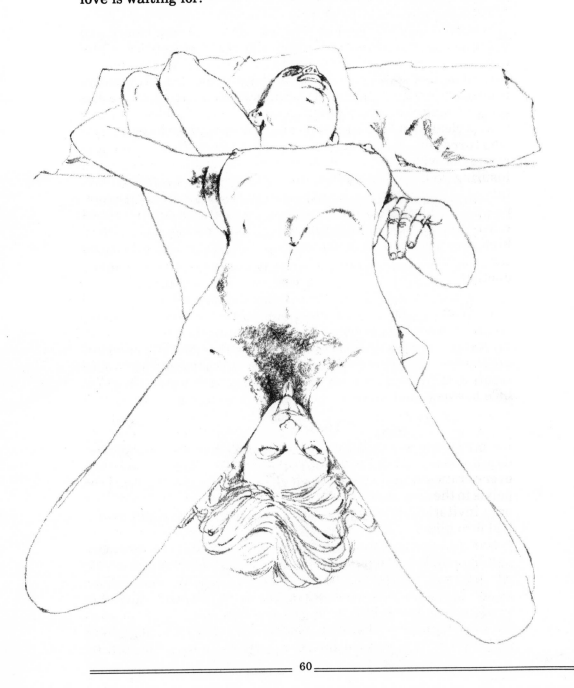

Crushes A crush is an innocuous fantasy that can enliven everyday experience and sometimes increase your enjoyment of the woman you really love. Crushes can also inspire—to poetry, to redecorating your apartment, to somehow "bettering" yourself. They can also, at times, help you to reinspect your *real* life, to get in better touch with new or revived needs, to reach a more realistic acceptance of what is.

However, crushes can also be a means of escaping reality and perpetually living in an as-if world. If fantasies supersede or preclude your engaging in actual relationships, best discover (through careful soul-searching or perhaps with the aid of a professional counselor or psychotherapist) what need this string of crushes serves. Chances are that by lighting on the unattainable—a woman who is clearly in love with someone else, some friend or associate who turns you on physically but whom you know deep in your guts would (for whatever reason) never be a compatible lover—you are insuring your own distancing from the demands imposed by close interaction. While there is nothing wrong with this from the standpoint of harming others (unless you allow your crush to make you a nuisance), you are cutting yourself off from the most meaningful kind of relationship with another human being: that in which you care mutually, and express your intimacy in making love to one another.

Cunt Of late liberated from street language to become a new word in the private vocabulary of lesbian lovers to express sexual sentiment, as, "I can't wait to get my mouth around your delicious cunt!" Like "dyke," typically used by men to insult women by attempting to reduce all of female meaning to the hole between their legs.

Dancing If dancing didn't exist, lesbians would invent it. If there is such a thing as foreplay for lesbians, dancing is it; within the dance, between lovers or potential lovers, every erotic possibility is ritualized, from the forward thrust of the pelvis to the slow rhythmic turn to display the ass. Hands signal not only invitation but suggestions of what they will perform in bed. Old formalized dances such as the tango and the rumba take on a peculiar erotic distinction when they are done by lesbians: a singular pattern emerges when four breasts instead of two are involved, when there is a subtle exchange of who leads in the middle of the dance. Fast non-touching dances are for body display, but lesbians typically will maintain direct eye contact during such performances, the eyes discussing what will, if anything, happen when the dance is done. Lesbians refined the sexual coding inherent in dancing

perhaps because more direct communication/invitation has for so long been dangerous in some cases, implicitly prohibited in most; the gay folklore built around "it takes one to know one" can be wrong. Even in today's liberal sexual climate, a woman who agrees to dance with you may be horrified at your suggestion that she also get in bed with you. A lesbian, dancing, may ask with her body and her eyes, but her partner must take the responsibility of signaling during the dance whether afterwards her partner will get what she is asking for.

Dancing between long-time lovers is one of the most reliable forms of reawakening sexual interest, especially if they go out dancing in a place where the dance floor is specifically and blatantly geared—through the music, the lighting, the decor—toward sexual arousal. Nearly all sizable cities have such places, some of them exclusively lesbian, others mixed gay and lesbian; increasingly, there are dance palaces built on recognition of bisexuality, where two women dancing together among mixed couples is the norm. For years, many lesbians had to fight back a feeling of shyness before they could ask another one to dance. Such shyness was based on "transgression" of male prerogative, on assumption of that prerogative. Happily, the breakdown in sex-role stereotyping has rendered such feelings in lesbians practically obsolete.

Dancing privately is always a sexual approach. Frequently there's hardly a distinction to be made between the dancing and the sex. Lovers strip themselves or each other to music, never stopping the momentum of the dance. When half naked, they kiss and caress the breasts or dance with just the nipples touching. You can slip your hands into her pants and cup her buttocks; bring your thigh against her vulva for a slow grind; manipulate the clitoris; slip a finger into her vagina or anus. It is difficult to engage in mutual lovemaking when dancing, but possible.

Demitasse The "little cup" you drink from as it lowers itself to your mouth.

Deodorants Over the past decade, readers of medical journals have noted far more articles describing the various irritations that can be caused by vulvar "deodorants" than the manufacturers have devised brands. A common ingredient is hexachlorophene, a methylene-chlorophenol preparation that is basically a detergent—frequently used for "scrubbing up" before surgery and scrubbing operating tables afterwards. Clean one should be, but that clean?

Of course, both the profits of industry and the protestations of nothing-womanly-can-be-bad arguers aside, a day's collection of sweat, natural vaginal secretions and less-than-fresh panties can render any woman's crotch far from kissable. We suggest soap and water, with plenty of rinsing (soap, too, can be an irritant). If that's impractical on occasion you might want to use one of the cleansing wipes available specifically for cleansing the outer vaginal and/or anal areas.

Underarm odor problems are perhaps more easily dealt with. To summarize what we said under *Armpits*, women respond to odors associated with lovemaking, but the smell of armpit sweat does not seem to rank high among them. Better safe than sorry—at least until you know each other better, and feel free to share your feelings about this often touchy area, and especially if (by virtue of your own sensitive nose and its testing of heavily stained clothing) you know your armpits do not exude a scent apt to evoke erotic responses in most human beings.

Discipline   "Discipline" is a euphemism for beating each other as a means of getting off or, at least, getting turned on. Understandably, the technique does not enjoy much popularity in lesbian circles because most women are fully aware of the falseness of the venerable myth that females like to be beaten. It also has links to the notion of martyrdom, which is a condition that most women want to flee, not foster.

In point of fact—except for those individuals who actually are sexually stimulated by the forceful application of sauna twigs, paddles, or whips—most people (women and men, gay or straight) actually respond most to the fantasy of it. Using nothing more fierce than the peacock feathers you use for *La plume de ma tante*, both of you may get a kick out of playing mistress–slave, Christian –lion, good mummy–bad child, or any number of other scenes you may devise to add more variety to your love-life. But if it doesn't feel right, don't do it. And don't ever try it when you're angry and really would like to beat up on your lover; that's an occasion for talking through, not acting out.

Display   Exposing oneself in public is a pastime outside the purview of most women, gay or straight. It is not just more difficult for women than for men, there is a psychological difference too, a desire to be less public about one's sexuality, being wont to seek love more than sex. There is also the matter of rebelling against the role of sex-object.

Nonetheless, divorced from its dirty-old-man connotations, a certain degree of exhibitionism is natural, universal and fun. If you know you have unusually good-looking breasts you are careful on a date to wear a shirt that shows them off to best advantage. If you are proud of your flat stomach you wear skin-tight pants that show your prominent hip bones and, if you are lucky, your high, slender ass too at their most provocative.

Real display belongs in the bedroom and means stripping to excite, not to tease. If that kind of display is ruled out because of a lack of personal confidence a real erotic advantage is lost.

Drag To wear drag is to dress flagrantly in clothing normally reserved for the opposite sex. With the collapse of rigid role-playing among lesbians, however, drag as such is on the decline. But where pockets of role-playing still exist (generally in big-city ghettos, in small towns, and among lesbians who choose not to change with the times) drag flourishes still.

The first women to put on trousers, however, were not necessarily lesbians, although many probably were; nor were they cross-dressing to show sexual temperament so much as to gain access to the money, adventure and mobility denied females. Some of these women became legends in their own time; others are remembered in folklore. Hannah Snell, heroine of British popular ballads in the eighteenth century, served as a "man" in the army and the navy. Commended for her bravery, she was even treated for the wounds she sustained in battle without her true sex being discovered. Loreta Velasquez enlisted in the Confederate Army to serve in the Civil War, fought at the battle of Bull Run, and was decorated (as a man) by General Stonewall Jackson. As pirates, thieves, warriors, highwaymen and professionals, generations of women have "passed" and successfully escaped the usual social and economic restrictions placed on women. All have had in common a strong drive for independence and survival in a man's world.

Some or all of these reasons are common among women who choose lesbianism and many women have successfully impersonated men primarily to make love to women. Counting on the maiden's sexual innocence, the pitch-dark of the bedroom and deftness with dildos, some impersonators have even accomplished legal marriages —and long and happy ones.

But now there are subtler nuances of meaning associated with the use of drag among women, entailing the adoption of exaggeratedly "feminine" attire: spike heels, tight skirts, lavish makeup, long fingernails, bouffant hair styles. Typically these women have rejected contemporary liberation movements (or been unaware of them) and find psychological and sexual satisfaction in passivity, submission and heterosexual game-playing as outmoded as their dress. Oddly enough, in the context of our times, lesbians who assume the opposite "masculine" role have the edge in terms of general mental health. Unconscious though they sometimes are of their costume's symbolism, women who wear starched white shirts, neckties, even pin-striped suits, are expressing a need to control their own lives, looking for places to put ambition and energy, wishing for the power accorded to men. Sophisticated play with drag among lesbians, however, is quite another matter and seldom has any sexual role expression.

Dressed sex Dressed sex means getting off with your clothes still on. It means rubbing pelvises and assuming a crotch-to-thigh position with a dancing partner; it is absent-mindedly (or consciously) crossing your legs and exercising your vaginal muscles as you while away time on a bus (see *Tribadism*).

More adventuresomely, there is toe-fucking under a restaurant table where the tablecloth is long enough to permit some discretion; (see *Big toe*). Crowded highways are a common site for starting doing each other by hand, although it is necessary to pull off the road pretty early on. Dressed sex is also useful for taking the edge off desire when you are dying to make love but dinner guests are expected at any moment.

Although "real" sex—nude and unrestricted as to time or techniques—is better, manipulating each other through clothing can be quite satisfying. The restrictions and the urgency give dressed sex a spice of the illicit, which can heighten excitement and facilitate orgasm (at least a "small" one) with very little effort.

If the situation permits, loosening a waistline will usually allow access to vulvar flesh. While the lovemaking hand can't move with such agility as in nudity, the technique is sometimes preferable to working through a layer of denim. Of course, partial disrobing makes closer contact—including mouthwork—possible, but then it's hardly dressed sex.

Dressed-sex approaches can open your eyes to heretofore unimagined "quickies." For example, otherwise tedious airplane flights can be marvelously enlivened under cover of a lap blanket. This is made easier if you are wearing earphones, so that people nearby, who are probably engaged in watching a movie or playing their own games, assume your grunts and giggles are in response to the channel of your preference.

Drugs Not wishing to rely unduly on our own observations, clinical and personal, we undertook an informal but fairly extensive survey, particularly among younger lesbians. It seems that relatively few are into the heavy drug scene. Those who were are out of it, and it's considered rather gauche to go much beyond smoking joints. At least for the present, pill-popping seems to be *out* of vogue while amyl nitrite ("poppers") is very much *in*.

It seems fairly obvious that lesbians do not exist in some special drug-free culture, though as with alcohol and sex, sometimes it's better to choose than to mix. A little grass can make every side look greener, but if your lover gets sick or passes out you are left with your own altered sensations. A little amyl nitrite can act as a neat catalyst to other chemical reactions, but while a number of gay women who do enjoy poppers enjoy them best as an accompaniment to music, many use them as a sexual response heightener.

As to the heavier stuff, don't. If you must experiment, save it for an occasion other than serious lovemaking with someone you really care about. Otherwise your lullaby can be someone else's nightmare (and vice versa), and since successful sharing is what good lovemaking is all about, allowing yourself (and/or your partner) to be zapped out of contact can amount to destroying a relationship.

Dyke Almost always a put-down when used by straights, especially by straight men, and particularly by straight men who fear a lesbian challenge to their masculinity. Among lesbians the word has traditionally been synonymous with "butch," connoting aggressive, "masculine" role-playing. Recently, however, "dyke" has taken on more positive associations, expressing pride, independence, assertiveness, liberation from heterosexist stereotyping: a pejorative turned inside out and used as a compliment. Also "bull dyke," "bull dagger," suggesting extremes of strength (or threat); "dykelet," "baby dyke" for the young or just-out lesbian; "bar dyke" for the lesbian who'd rather be in a bar than in a bed.

Ears Who said Latin and Greek are dead languages? Whispered gently into the ear you are fingering, kissing, tonguing, and gently nibbling, it can send hot chills right down to your lover's *vulva*. As your tongue slides nimbly down along the *helix*, then back up the *anti-helix* and *scapula*, try fingering the *concha* before you nibble the *tragus*, tongue the *fossa triangularis*, and suck (fairly hard) on the *lobule*. With your lips protruding goldfish style to encircle the *external meatus*, softly whisper that she has the sexiest *anti-tragus* you've ever seen and how, if you could just shrink to elfin size, you would like to curl up and rest blissfully in her *intertragic notch*.

If she's not enchanted, she's most apt to giggle—and that's O.K. because fun and foolishness belong in sex.

Two notes of caution: never talk, yell or moan loudly into your partner's ear (it hurts and can affect hearing) and test out whether your lover likes ear play: some women are hypersensitive to wetness in the ear and find it more distracting than stimulating.

Eyes Eyes are probably the recipients of more love poetry than any other part of the female anatomy. Lesbian eyes, however, don't just lie there waiting to be admired. Second only to hands and mouths, lesbian eyes are active participants in lesbian sexuality, incapable—like the true-to-life lesbian herself—of being sentimentalized. Lesbian eyes seduce with a direct, unflinching gaze that, alone, can bring their object to a limp-kneed state of sexual arousal. Lesbian eyes cruise: they can give a stranger's body an instant's worth of intimacy as effective, for some, as a night's worth of lovemaking. Lesbian eyes, for these reasons, are sometimes covered—especially at night—with sunglasses, which for generations have been the ultimate lesbian armor against too much self-revelation, too much exposure of feeling.

Fantasy A waking dream in which a sexual wish is perfectly imagined and perfectly gratified. A sexual fantasy may consist of no more than a split-second image caused by brief sensory impact: a smell, a stranger's face, a particular sound— any of which could awaken erotic memory or stimulate erotic hope. Or a sexual fantasy may be a lifelong process, begun in early adolescence and built upon with increasingly intricate detail, theatrical furnishings, changing characters: an entire "secret life" energizing and enriching the dreamer's mind–body connections. Certainly, sexual fantasy is almost always accompanied by masturbation or used for self-excitation during sexual contact with another. To act out the fantasy with another, however, is almost always a disappointment: no reality can compete with dream's ideal.

Not unremarkably, lesbian erotic fantasies are often based on heroism, which is, of course, sexually rewarded in just measure. For instance, you are a knight in shining armor, plunging on your noble steed through a pack of villains to save the lady in distress—and the lady looks exactly like the waitress at your favorite lunchtime restaurant, except now, in your fantasy, she is draped in breast-bearing medieval velvet instead of that ghastly nylon uniform. You know she is waiting for a hero in a Wall Street suit to rescue her from the restaurant and you know you're that hero. You also know what would happen should you indicate this fact to her: a bowl of soup in your lap and a shriek of horror. So you have her in your mind—and satisfy both your sexual need and your heroic dream. . . . The serum you devised saves the city from plague—and your nurse falls naked into your arms. . . . You battle, single-handedly, the monster from outer space—and then make love to your impossibly blonde heroine under the moonlit jungle vines. . . . Before the crowned heads of Europe and the entire, cheering population of your home town, all of whom said you could never do it, you are presented with a Nobel Prize—and for the rest of the night a dozen Swedish movie stars take turns sucking champagne off your clitoris while your arch-enemies are forced to watch.

Because lesbians are women, they have been socially diverted from action in much of the "real world's" theaters. But more than other women, lesbians need action and the rewards given for successful action, mainly the praise and love of women. Hence intellectual and fantasy action, the target of fame and glory as well as endless orgasm. Fantasy is *not*, to say the least, the most sophisticated form of mental activity.

Much lesbian fantasy can have embarrassingly heterosexual features of the me-Tarzan, you-Jane variety described above. Or, even more shamefully to some very hard-core dykes, the favorite sexual fantasy may be me-Jane, you-Tarzan. Indeed, the more active the life (the more responsible, hard-working, commanding) the more passive the dreamer's role in her fantasy. The reason for this should be obvious and should clear away all vestiges of shame: you need a rest; you need, for a change, to be seduced and pampered; you need to give in and to give over sexually. While your pride and any number of other psychological factors may make such a rest impossible in your real sexual life, the fantasy vacation you give yourself may be critical to your continuing mental health—and will reward you indirectly by pouring energy into your other life of achievement and action if you understand why you are doing it, if you let yourself have the fantasy without shame. If, too, sometimes your places-of-rest fantasies involve a man, you should regard them in the same light. We enact in fantasy not only physical impossibilities but also psychological impossibilities; intercourse with a man, for many lesbians, is one of them. Dreaming away the impossible clears the mind, as well as the life, for the real.

Feminism and lesbianism Feminism and lesbianism are both, at their simplest, about women loving women. The intellectual, physical, spiritual and political forms this love has taken are as varied in shape and purpose as there are women to love and be loved.

For most lesbians, feminism comes naturally and easily. Lesbians live daily by the principles on which feminism is predicated, practicing the most fundamental of them without a second thought—women come first and should continue to come first, at least until the awful imbalance of opportunity, privilege and choice between men and women is righted. A lesbian feminist is a woman (straight or gay) who believes that none of the world's inequities, from class and racial injustices to food distribution, can be cured without first recognizing that the primary model for these injustices is male domination over women. Some lesbians, either temporarily or permanently discouraged with feminist efforts to re-educate and transform the system, advocate complete separation from men and their institutions and from straight women—and from lesbians who do not agree with separatist ideology. Some lesbians, at the other end of the spectrum, continue to work genially and constructively with their local chapter of the National Organization for Women or one of the other broadly based national groups. Most, however, eventually begin to concentrate application of feminist ideas to those areas of their lives in which they have the most expertise and training: if a woman is a musicologist she seeks to recover lost compositions by women and to encourage the expression of lesbian sensibility in new composers; if she is in business, she actively seeks to employ and promote qualified women; if a teacher, she makes room in her research and course planning for women's history, literature, philosophy.

In personal terms, feminism has been the most catalytic agent in freeing lesbians from old fears and self-doubt, from internalized rage, from the external pressures to hide and to conform to the heterosexual version of reality. Especially in the past ten years those lesbians who have achieved the most in their fields, who are the most sexually active, who wield the most power among both men and women are also feminists. The old caricature of the snarling bluestocking has by and large been supplanted by the image of a woman who is coveted for her independence, for her calculated risk-taking and for her ability to love herself. Feminism has given the lesbian more ways to show her love for more women.

Fidelity If you are lucky enough to have a stable, rather long-standing relationship with another woman you love, respect and enjoy, then you naturally have the responsibility of considering her as well as yourself when you engage in any sort of behavior that might threaten to damage that relationship. It is a matter of negotiating with each other until you arrive at a mutually acceptable hierarchy of priorities. Some lesbians feel so secure in their relationship that occasional straying (on either lover's part) causes no real concern. Other women—even some who feel equally secure in their relationship—will be hurt, angry, depressed or even panicked. In between those extremes is a wide range of reaction, with a midline of tolerating the situation but not being very happy about it.

Again, the crucial point is to talk about it, preferably before it happens. Explain your stance, listen to hers. See what common elements exist. Try to combine all this in a negotiated decision that seems reasonable and understandable to you both. Don't be surprised if it fails to work, but take heart in knowing that the reaction would have been much more severe had you never had the discussion.

And don't neglect discretion. In an era in which we've all been brainwashed—largely, but not entirely, because of the influence of the more up-front, encounter-type forms of psychotherapy—to "tell it like it is," many people open up, vomit it out and leave the hapless listener with not one shred of ego left. It's done in the name of honesty, but it is actually an act of aggression against the lover's integrity and a method of expiating one's own sense of guilt.

Fingers Typically, the talk goes this way: "If God/Nature had intended that there be any kind of sex other than heterosex, he/she would not have designed woman with a vagina and man with a penis to put into that vagina." While fitting

pieces of the human puzzle together may be the prime function of reproduction, it is not necessarily the case in bringing off female sexual pleasure. The lesbian counter-argument might go: "If Goddess/Nature had intended that there be any kind of sex other than lesbianism, she/she would not have designed women with vaginas and with fingers that reach exactly to the point where a vagina may be stroked to maximum pleasure." In short, the vagina has sensory receptors only at its opening, the *introitus*—just about a finger's length up into it. If a woman has had no lesbian experience at all— even if she has never heard the word "lesbian"—blind instinct alone will cause her initially to make love with her fingers. It has been suggested that the practiced lesbian hand, in its agility and in its capacity to call forth the most precise nuances of sexual pleasure in a woman, is comparable to the hands of concert pianists and violinists and, if sexual performers were taken as seriously as concert performers, should carry the same amount of insurance. Lesbians cruise each other's fingers, in the same fashion perhaps that straight women speculate on the lump beneath a man's fly.

Finishing off Shorthand (tongue, foot, thigh, dildo, vibrator) for bringing someone to orgasm. Often used in the context of "giving it" to a lover half crazed from desire built up from long lovemaking, or as an end to drawn-out lovemaking which, rather than getting off, was the primary objective in itself.

Flagellation Flagellation is an erotic speciality so uncommon among lesbians that if it exists at all it springs from extra-lesbian sexual desire. Most imaginative literature about flagellation is based on a male fantasy about being whipped by an enraged woman. Flagellation as a religious exercise —to drive out evil spirits, to punish the sinful body—has been its other use historically. Both experiences are apparently capable of producing, in the flagellant, sexual ecstasy through pain. The wish for pain as an ingredient of pleasure, however, is seldom the same thing as the literal experience of pain. If you have fantasies of being whipped by a lovely/ugly, young/old, naked/clothed (and so forth) woman it's a good idea to do some careful self-searching and determine the origin of such fantasies before you actually set up a situation where they can be acted out. It is generally understood that the greater the sexual excitement—particularly as orgasm is approached—the greater the tolerance of pain. To seek pain as the object of sexual activity, however, requires first of all the choice of a partner who is not into violence herself and who is *not* going to accommodate your fantasy to the letter: what turns you on in your mind may very easily be a turn-off in practice; furthermore, it may hurt like hell.

If you've decided to try it, these cautions are based on common sensuous sense. The first and fundamental requirement is to have a partner whom you know and trust—not a stranger whom you've had five martinis with in some bar and who appears more than willing to go home with you and give you what you want. Second, try out the fantasy for the first time with whips that can do no damage, such as cotton or silk sashes. Don't immediately rush out and buy a leather razor-strop similar to the one your father may have punished you with. The simple pantomime of flagellation with something soft may be enough to convince you that your wish to be whipped is coming from some place other than sexual need. If, however, pain proves to be a pleasure stimulus, both you and your partner should keep in mind that the object of the beating is to produce a tantalizing rhythm of strokes with essential elements of surprise and teasing. Cruelty and force are not what the fantasizer has in mind, no matter what she says. "Delicious torment" is the name of the game, and the object is her orgasm.

Most flagellants see themselves tied up during the whipping: being utterly helpless in the hands of the tormentor appears to be an essential part of the fantasy. Use bonds, however, that don't hurt or leave burns on the ankles and wrists. Again, keep with the cotton/silk category and stay clear of leather manacles (see *Bondage*). Talk, of course, is the real turn-on in this event and in talk is where the real brutality should remain, with the whipper (as she ties up her "victim") detailing the causes of the punishment and suggesting what she intends to do; the flagellant typically is pleading for mercy. Use sauna twigs if you can get them or peacock feathers, willow-tree wands, pussy-willow branches [*sic*] if you can't. The flagellant should be tied in a spreadeagle position, with her vulva open and vulnerable to the switches. Again, remember that rhythm, surprise and talk are what build the pleasure, not wild attack. If she's really into it, orgasm should happen with a few delicately applied strokes to the vulva.

Foreplay For most women foreplay is not just something you do before "really" making love, it is a major part of really making love. All the caressing, whispering, stroking, kissing, undressing, close embraces, fingers-through-hair, breast stimulation, and what-you-will form more than a prelude to genital contact. They combine to orchestrate a series of climaxes that are totally enjoyable in and of themselves. In fact, rushing obsessively toward the grand finale can rob you both of sharing all those sensual delights women seem instinctively to know about and which, they have been complaining for centuries, men customarily ignore in their haste to screw. Women really do seem to know better.

The joy of sex for lesbians is that sex is not just screwing, but all the other delicious components of communicating sensuality in a framework that combines tenderness and passion not bounded by the crotch.

Frequency of sex There is, dear reader, no Great Lesbian In The Sky keeping a record of how often you do it.

Frequency is to sex as taste is to vichyssoise: some like it hot, some like it cold. Some lesbian lovers, especially at first in the electric waves of lust and romance, make love two, three, four, or more times daily. Some lesbian lovers, especially later on in the comfort and security of middle-aged domesticity, seem to take satisfaction in one or two sexual excursions each week. Although median frequency may be something in between, it's impossible to arrive at any meaningful average for all lesbians at all times.

The unattached lesbian may masturbate several times a week. Then again, she may not. Sex with other people could for her be a bimonthly event or perhaps involve a weekly assignation.

Some lesbian couples—especially some of those caught up in the publish-or-perish syndrome many ambitious, productive women are—find the daily hassle too enervating to allow for the sense of fun and freedom that should accompany sex. So they often tend to "save up" for, say, an overnight stay at a motel. Change of scene can enliven anyone's sex life.

The most important aspect of frequency of sex as it concerns a loving couple is that it be mutually satisfying. If you want more and she wants less be sure that this is openly discussed. Keep in mind that neither of you is "right" or "wrong"; the goal is to negotiate some compromise that feels good to both of you.

The introduction (or extended use) of some toys—vibrators, dildos, feathers, ice cubes, what-have-you—can help in several ways: relief for the less sexy, fulfillment for the more sexy, and creation of a more lively and adventuresome ambience that may rouse both of you to intensified pleasure.

Another important thing to remember is that no one's preference for frequency of sex is set in a fixed pattern. You may, for example, go along accepting your current frequency as entirely satisfactory and then hit a week when sheer lust molds the focus and structure of every minute. You are insatiable, wanting to make love morning, noon and night, yet your friend, usually more turned-on than you, has suddenly become engrossed in learning the markings of every bird inhabiting the continent of North America, east of the Rocky Mountains. She sits clutching an illustrated guidebook to birds as you clutch your throbbing crotch. That's when you need a shared sense of humor, which is a vital prerequisite to all good sex.

Finally, and this is another difficulty about averages (is once one week and then five times the next week three per week?), never schedule sex. If you make love once daily, be sure it's not just at night, before going to sleep; try mornings, or an occasional lunchtime break. If you make love once weekly, be absolutely certain that you don't fall into a now's-the-day rut. Remember also that sexual drive lessens more from lack of activity than from age (see *Growing older*). If you want to ensure happy sex in your "golden years" keep the juices flowing with as much lovemaking as you and your partner agree suits you both. If you're alone, masturbate as often as the urge strikes you.

Friendship Lesbians frequently speak of their lover as "my friend." This is not evasion but the honest truth, because women, both gay and straight, tend to think of a lover not so much as someone to have sex with but as someone to care for, share with, communicate with, cuddle, be devoted to, play with, confide in, believe in, enjoy life with, grow with, and participate in a mutual dedication. In short, a friend. Lovemaking is then a wondrous and treasured bonus, but not the be-all and end-all.

In friendship there is both acceptance and understanding—a willingness to tolerate idiosyncrasies, support the other person's separateness and integrity and forgive trespasses. In short, friendship is love—a very special kind of love, and it is that which is the touchstone of lesbianism. The lesbian wants to make love to her friend not just to take her or to get off herself, but because to sexualize a loving friendship is to make a good thing even better.

It's interesting to note how many lesbians maintain two- and three-decade friendships with women who have long ceased to be their lovers. Evidently friendship can withstand desexualization just as well as it can sexualization.

Frigidity A condition simply unheard of among lesbians. We include it here primarily to dispel a few more myths about the nature of female sexuality in general and lesbian sexuality in particular. The term of course connotes coldness, an incapacity (or an unwillingness) to respond sexually, an inability to heat up, to achieve orgasm.

The psychosexual meaning of frigidity as it is usually employed is, once again, based on the assumption that woman's primary sexual relationship is with a penis. Certainly that was Freud's assumption when, in differentiating between two kinds of orgasm in females, he declared that clitoral orgasm (which does not require a penis) is "immature" and vaginal orgasm (which he rather unimaginatively assumed is always brought about by the insertion of a real live penis) is "mature." Freud's judgment on female orgasm had the cultural effect of throwing a considerable number of heterosexual women into tailspins of anxiety over their sexual health and "maturity." One imagines quite a few of these women practically anesthetizing their clitorises and grinding away on some exhausted penises for hours hoping for the Viennese Papa's approval. Lesbians, of course, suffered even more from Freud's disqualification of the clitoris as a socially approved site of orgasm and, even while the steam was pouring from their eyeballs from clitoral orgasm, believed in their heads that "mature womanhood" would be forever denied them until their vaginas could somehow make friends with a penis. "Frigidity" therefore has taken on the cultural meaning of being incapable of achieving vaginal orgasm with a penis.

The physiological facts of the matter were always there and always ignored: while (as every lesbian knows) clitoral orgasm can be achieved without vaginal stimulation, "vaginal orgasm" is impossible to achieve without clitoral stimulation. The vagina simply doesn't have the requisite sensory receptors and the clitoris is for nothing but sexual sensation. Probably the entire enigma of female "frigidity" can, like so many other female problems, be explained by the male inability to imagine that women can get along (and often better) without the sacred penis. If lesbians experience "frigidity" they are experiencing lousy lovemaking and/or boredom with a lover. Such is generally the case for straight women, too.

Fucking It's taken more than half a century to dissipate the absurd notion (to which the early psychoanalysts lent their authority) that the vagina is the "real" place of orgasm in women. Now that surely everybody is satisfied it's the clitoris that counts, the pendulum is swinging toward a more balanced position.

That is, while no one—least of all lesbians—doubts that clitoral stimulation is the *sine qua non* of a rich, full orgasm, a growing number of gay women are discovering (or rediscovering) that the sensation of fullness in the vagina lends a special dimension to lovemaking. Many lesbians, in fact, are not totally satisfied with sex unless vaginal fullness plays a major part and fewer, now, are regarding fucking as an aping of straight sex—that is, as if fucking were synonymous with the action of a man's penis inside a woman. As with so many other things, lesbians are learning that fucking is not only a man's prerogative conferred by virtue of his anatomy. Fucking is another human sexual activity with its own spectrum of need, performance and accomplishment and one, for lesbians, with many variations.

From the standpoint of what you actually *do*, fucking is very

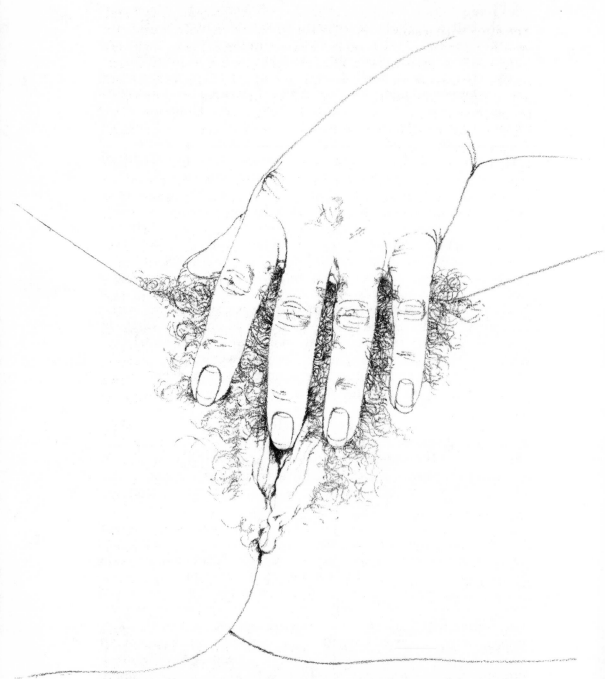

similar to masturbation: loving yourself frequently leads to fucking yourself. When you're with another you love you already know what feels good, how it feels good; and you can imagine (because she is built just like you) how the pleasure is going to be doubled.

The most common method of women fucking women is by hand. You start with a slow stroking of the whole vulva. With the palm of your hand resting lightly on her bush, your fingers take back-and-forth excursions in and out, around and about her moistening lips. As she arouses to your touch, you begin to circle the clitoris, but with a feather touch of the thumb while your fingers are insinuating themselves at the vaginal opening. Sometimes two hands are better than one: kneeling by her vulva you work one hand on the clitoris, the other on the vagina.

Either way your lover should be indicating by this time just how much vaginal penetration she desires. Whether she uses words or motions or noises, you will learn to read what her pleasure is as your fingers are learning to stroke that pleasure to life. You will also learn the amount of thickness she wants inside her and the times when she may want more or less. Depending on her need for fullness and on the pitch of her excitement and wetness, she may vary between wanting one, two or three fingers fucking her. Knitting your forefinger and middle finger together, or all three middle fingers together, works well, particularly for those who enjoy hard, deliberate fucking. The forefinger or middle finger is best for light, rapid in-and-out stroking. Again, while your fingers concentrate on the vagina, your thumb is free to play with the clitoris and she is free to move against or from your thumb's pressure as she follows your rhythm. Too much clitoral pressure too soon may inhibit your lover's orgasm.

There are two basic hand positions for finger fucking. With the *upward hand* position (that is, with the back of your wrist and your hand nearest the perineum and/or anus), your thumb has more freedom of action for the clitoris while your fingers work the vagina. Also, more penetration is usually possible from this angle. If you (or your lover) wish, you can switch from this position to the *downward hand* position (the back of your wrist and hand above her vulva) without losing contact by simply (but carefully) rotating your hand. Speaking of rotation, many women enjoy a circling, grooving movement inside the vagina (it can be increased to a quick vibrato at the onset of orgasm) as well as the in-and-out thrust.

Necessity is often the mother of invention when it comes to "positions." If, for example, you weigh 120 and your lover 180, you may find that a side-by-side, face-to-face position, with your lover's knee hooked up as far as she can get it, is most comfortable. This position is also excellent for simultaneous fucking, providing both partners can reach each other's vulvas. And provided that you've taught your left (or right) hand what the other one knows already.

While exploring the possibilities of simultaneous fucking, you can keep in mind that centuries-old invention, probably the most significant aid ever devised for sex between women, the double-headed dildo. If you or your lover have any reservations about trying this miracle of ancient science (confusing it in your mind with a penis) you can free yourself up for its delight by remembering its non-male attributes: that it offers the only method of simultaneous fucking that frees all four hands for caressing and holding and allows full body contact; that it is always erect; that it transmits neither sperm nor disease—only pleasure when you want it; above all, it belongs to *both* of you. Many manufacturers of the dildo, however, have not yet got their grip on female reality and are still producing on the basis of "the bigger the better." Some of the longer double-headed dildos sport a circumference few women would find stimulating or even comfortable. One, however, measures just slightly more than 4 inches around and is 12 inches long. If you're sufficiently agile and not too chubby you'll find this size satisfactory, although a greater length (up to a limit) will permit a greater variety of positions.

These molded plastic dildos are stiff, yet pliable. They are washable and can be stored in a clean sock (or a silk stocking: as you please!) under the pillow. In the spirit of fun-and-games that makes for better sex, many lesbians fool around with their dildo (throwing it around like a ball, rubbing it on the skin, wearing it in their panties, etc.) as a playtime turn on.

When you're ready to get down to business, the sky's the limit. Here, too, the side-by-side position is especially good, particularly if one of you has any lingering doubts about assuming any traditionally "straight" (e.g. the missionary) position. This requires getting so close to one another you're practically inside your lover's skin, while you both hold on tight and mutually grind/thrust with the pelvis. Or, one partner may wish to kneel over the other, either straddling her or with knees between knees; you may decide to reverse mid-fuck, holding tightly to each other's buttocks as you effect the rollover.

Many lesbians find watching their lover masturbate under any circumstances overwhelmingly erotic and seeing her slip the dildo in and out of herself while you wait, to join in or take over, has its special inspirations. You can sit beside her as she inserts her end of the dildo into her own vagina. Then you can sit between her legs, vulva to vulva, and insert your end into you. While this position affords little body contact, it leaves the hands free to caress and squeeze each other's thighs, bellies, breasts, clitorises. Or, by slipping one leg under each other's and turning a bit sideways ("scissors" position) you may be able to achieve some clitoris-to-clitoris contact while you fuck.

Introducing a vibrator into a dildo-fucking scene can be a pleasurable plus. All it requires is that you assume a position, with the double dildo inside both of you, that leaves space between your bodies for the vibrator's work on both clitorises. For some women, the touch of the vibrator in this instance can mean immediate orgasm. If this is the case for you, but not your partner, move back a little, holding the vibrator against her and manipulating it until she comes.

Finally, even the tightest-working muscles may lose a dildo, especially when it is basically too short for two women moving in a tempo of sexual excitement. When this happens, as it sometimes will, you simply use one of the four available hands to keep the vagrant end inside and working.

Some obvious cautions: Have some care about the angle and depth of penetration until you're both accustomed to the double dildo. Keep the dildo clean: after you use it (or, at least as soon as you wake up) scrub it with soap and water and rinse well. Stick to your end of the dildo—a possible vaginal irritation is *not* what you want to transmit in fucking.

Gentleness The old sex manuals devoted a lot of space to instructing men on being "gentle" to their brides— touch softly, kiss lightly, thrust slowly (if at all), and mutter sweet nothings about love. Almost like one would treat a beloved pet.

"Gentle" derives from the Old French *gentil*, meaning "noble"; as in *nobless oblige*, man is obliged to be "generous" toward his inferior, woman. No one is sure whether women are inherently less "beast-like" and more gentle or whether their much proclaimed gentleness reflects different socialization patterns, but we are certain that the difference exists; hence to tell women to be gentle in their love-making with other women would be silly. Besides, being gentle implies caring, and caring, in the sense of making love as opposed to having sex, is the overall theme of this book.

Growing older   Women never have to worry about getting it up, so at an age when men begin to fret about difficulties with penile erection women's sexual equipment remains blissfully unimpaired. Not even menopause diminishes sexuality— in fact, it often increases it. For some women a kind of psychological block can occur, something along the lines of oh-my-gawd-I'm-no-longer-young, but since procreation has not played a dominant role in most lesbians' sex lives, the loss of potential fertility is not trau-matic. The only significant physical difference is that hormonal changes cause some women to complain of less lubrication than they had previously experienced, but a sensitive lover can easily correct that situation.

The fun thing about aging is that one gets to dump so much behavioral garbage. It is no longer necessary to engage in all the competitive, devious, aggressive and status-seeking activity stimu-lated by a society in which acquisition is a principal measure of being alive. It's time to relax.

Similarly, lovemaking may become calmer. Not less intense, and certainly not less meaningful, but calmer. Like skiing the same trails, but finding more adaptive ways of traversing or side-slipping.

Sallie, a 68-year-old retired physician, and Deborah, who will leave her teaching job when she turns 65 next spring, recently talked of spending all day Saturday in bed—making love from breakfast until it was too late to prepare dinner, so they called a home-delivery food service and continued to make love. They were not bragging about their prowess, nor is either of them given to publicly dis-cussing her sex life. The story was told with warmth and humor, rather as if to reassure younger lesbians (who frequently share straight people's misconceptions about sex after 50) and also to comment on how, in younger days, it was difficult to find time to make love all day.

For the woman without a partner, or who is temporarily separated from one, there can be only one source of release: masturbation. As long as you are alive, you are capable of—and "entitled" to—sexual arousal and satisfaction. An erogenous zone is something like a fine violin. Play it often and it keeps in tune. Put it away, forgotten in a case, and it comes unstrung.

If she is old and you are much younger, you can name in your lovemaking all the things that are cherished only when they are old—lace, wine, mahogany, oak trees, antique jewelry, the yellowing pages of ancient books. Bring into the environment as many of these beautiful old things as you can. Remember as you caress her that you are privileged to have in your arms a wise body that needs to be taught nothing. And relax completely in the certain knowledge that your own body will very soon be in the hands of a maestro.

If you are old and she is much younger, tell her at the start that you are good and old—don't let her say things like, "But you look so young," as if they were compliments. Choose an environment with as many beautiful old things as you can. Let her experience you as old—remember, she may well have loved her grandmother best of all women once. By your uninhibited pleasure in your own old age, you will release her from her own fears of growing old one day—and within that release she may experience the most joyous sex of her life. Be careful not to overdo it, though; you don't want to make her feel inadequate just because she is young.

Above all, always remember that there *is* sex after 50, or 60, 70, and even 80 if you're on that side of the actuarial tables which so favor women to begin with.

Hair The fad of shaving it off, apparently as a protest against male definitions of female hair as "sexy," encountered relatively little success in lesbian circles because women find it sexy too. Little wonder, when you consider its uses. Stroking your partner's hair can be as arousing to you as it is to her. Long hair teasingly brushes your shoulders and breasts as she leans over to kiss you in bed; short hair mingles and intertwines with your bush as she kisses the place where thigh joins torso. You bury yourselves against one another and run your fingers excitedly through each other's hair, fondling, twirling, rubbing, tousling, and then kissing swaths that lead to special places like the temple, the nape of the neck or behind the ear.

Almost like eyes and hands, hair is a signal. It may be the first part of her anatomy you smell and touch with your lips as you hug or dance. You like its clean freshness; you find yourself musing about its color; you wonder why you always found blonde hair so appealing when, clearly, jet black is so much more exotic (or vice versa). You may even find yourself—as lovers have for centuries—wanting a locket of her hair. You like her hair cropped short, so you can enjoy the shape of her head; you like her hair long because you are excited by the way she tosses her head to rearrange it.

Enjoying your lover's hair is such a natural part of being in love that we seriously recommend asking her how she feels if you contemplate having it hacked off, straightened or frizzed. Obviously, it's your hair, you have the right to fix it as you wish and if she "really" loves you she won't mind anyway. But it's one of those thoughtful courtesies that mean you also take her into consideration. Besides, her perception of how you look just might be better than yours.

Handicapped lesbians Handicapped lesbians are not handicapped by their lesbianism, but their lesbianism can be handicapped by their handicap.

How do you get that wheelchair up the flight of stairs that leads to the newest, highly touted gay restaurant? How do you sign to that attractive woman who is obviously cruising you but who might mistake your halting speech for something other than deafness? How will she react when she discovers that there is no arm to slide into the sleeve of the jacket draped deftly over your shoulder?

Neither sexual drive nor the need for love and companionship are lacking in the physically handicapped, yet the pursuit of fulfillment can be devastatingly hampered both by fear of rejection and also by quite real problems in getting about, communicating with others and, of course, in some sexual acts. Nonetheless, the sexuality of the handicapped will not be denied and we applaud the efforts of the small but growing movement that is fighting to release the physically handicapped from the stigma of being "different." We can imagine few handicaps that in and of themselves could prevent lesbians from finding sexual satisfaction.

Holding out We are all for games— games of the sort that bring more joy to sex. Holding out is also a game, but quite joyless unless the player is sadistic and the playee masochistic.

The term "holding out" was invented by men to describe the activities of women they call "cock teasers"—women who would go only so far, and then refuse intercourse. In actuality there wasn't much choice for most women; holding out for wedding bells and a certificate was just about their only insurance on admission to a life-style they had been trained to believe was their lot. We suspect that with increasing liberation (of both sexes), somewhat less emphasis on marriage and more sophistication about birth control methods there is less holding out among straight women. We know that there is very little holding out among gay women; in fact, we've been unable to ascertain whether—except possibly in small pockets of rather outdated lesbianism where male–female role-playing still exists—there has ever been indulgence in the game. This is understandable. Lesbians pride themselves on the equality of their relationships; being free and independent, they need not fear that their sexual equipment is some secret prize that must be held in reserve for some dominant being to whom they will then submit for the trade-off of shelter and food.

If, however, one reads for holding out the concept of holding *back*— that is, not necessarily jumping into bed after a fifteen-minute acquaintance with some woman who attracts you—then certainly most lesbians would usually qualify. One of the great delights of being a woman is that you can make love at any time. Since you don't have to wait for an erection you can afford to wait for another evening, trusting that the romance of getting to know one another will only heighten the pleasure of your eventual lovemaking.

Horniness   Basically a straight term for feeling sexy. It probably derives from the hardness of the male organ when its owner is aroused. However, the term is also used by lesbians: "I'm horny" meaning "I feel sexier than usual."

Hugging   There are hugs you give children, hugs your mother gives you, hugs you give your best friend and then there are distinctive lesbian hugs that can mean something more than warm affection. Straight women, it has been observed, hug at the shoulders. Their arms grip each other's shoulder blades, their chins touch, their eyes look in opposite directions. From the shoulders down, their bodies make a diamond-shape which avoids breast and certainly pelvic contact. Behinds, in this position, linger uncertainly in space as though they have been orphaned from the rest of the body. Such a hug loudly announces "I am straight! And don't think I'm going to feel your body and have you think maybe I'm not. . . ."

A lesbian hug, even between women who have no intention of becoming lovers, is quite another matter. Two lesbians hugging is a vision of the solidarity of female flesh: arms wrap all the way around the back, fingers tuck themselves beneath the arms, breasts nuzzle together into a fit which feels perfect even if it is not; bellies flatten together. One pelvis feels the other pelvis. In a lesbian hug each woman takes the body-print of the other. The lesbian hug slips across the borderline from friendly embrace to sexual embrace when one opens her thighs at the nudging of the other's knee: whereupon the open thighs begin a special hug of their own, capturing the other thigh, tightening and feeling the pleasure of pressure against the vulva. The one whose thigh is captured in the hug can get almost the same amount of pressure by pulling her other leg around and about the other's accessible thigh. In this position, everything that can be hugged is getting hugged. If the enfolding arms stay wrapped around the backs, the breasts feel the most intense pressure. One woman may drop her arms and instead squeeze the buttocks in increasing pressure in the pelvic area. A nice, slow grind is, of course, accompanying this little hugging ballet.

Among the many very good reasons (including freedom of movement) lesbians have generally adopted pants-wearing is that it is almost impossible to pull off a good lesbian hug in a skirt.

Hysterectomy and oophorectomy The former refers to surgical removal of the uterus, the latter to surgical removal of an ovary (sometimes unilateral, sometimes bilateral). A hysterectomy can be performed through the abdominal wall or through the vagina; in some cases the operation can be "subtotal," leaving the cervix in place; in other instances the extent of pathology may dictate the "radical" procedure, where some of the vagina (along with some parametrial tissue) is excised.

Any surgical procedure is experienced as an insult to or violation of the body and one needs both inner strength and support from partners to combat the depression and feeling of helplessness that ensue. (If you've ever come home to a burgled apartment and felt that violation, try to imagine how it must feel to have something taken from inside your own body.)

However, your womanliness is *not* dependent upon your capacity to bear babies. Nor does your sexual responsiveness depend on the intactness of organs that are not the anatomical sites of lovemaking. Some women may experience hormonal imbalances that are easy to correct medically, but no woman need feel that she is less sexually desirable, for having had either of these operations.

If your lover should need such surgery, patiently help her to understand that you love *her*—not her ovaries or her uterus, or her appendix or nasal septum.

Intimacy Intimacy connotes the kind of closeness that allows you to speak your innermost thoughts, knowing that they will be fully accepted if not "understood."

Lesbians generally enjoy more intimacy than people in general. Why? They quickly learn that they cannot always rely on the goodwill of the external world, so they concentrate on their own heads— their sense of values, mores, attitudes, what is meaningful to them, life goals, what is pleasurable and what is painful. In short, how they wish to live.

This is not self-absorption, and it is antithetical to narcissism. It is the kind of inner-directed exploration that leads one to becoming outer-directed in the sense of relating to others, not just being in their company. Secure in your own sense of selfhood, you are able to accept the other person's selfhood. A lesbian knows and loves herself; she is then able to know and love someone else. She is open to intimacy and she usually finds it, not just with another woman she's in love with, but with a wide circle of friends she loves. Happily, her fruitful intimacy doesn't cause her to retire from society; indeed, she commonly works hard to effect changes that will benefit various groups of people striving to express their individuality within the societal structures people in general can subscribe to.

Jealousy   Jealousy is self-inflicted torture, caused by the mistaken assumption that it is possible to own and actively control another human being. Jealousy also has components of envy—when your lover chooses to have sex with another woman she is electing pleasure with someone other than you. Because jealousy derives from possessiveness it is the antithesis to all that belief in freedom you espouse—particularly, if you will, the freedom inherent in being a lesbian.

Jealousy is not "natural" to the human condition. It is an emotion we are subtly trained to feel so that we will more easily accommodate ourselves to heterosexual institutions (marriage, coupledom, the family): to love means to marry, to marry means to belong to each other forever.

Lesbians have had, as yet, little time to devise freeing alternatives to heterosexual systems that arouse self-destructive emotion. Until Utopia, however, the best way to deal with jealousy is to admit feeling it and try to effect some compromise that will not inhibit your lover's freedom of movement too severely and also release you from the obsession. If you are the object of a lover's jealousy, be especially careful not to turn that jealousy into a game. There can be perverse pleasure in being the cause of another's suffering, and in using that suffering to keep another in bondage.

Kissing   Kissing is the first plunge into physical intimacy, and it can be the ultimate act of knowledge and communion when it is engaged in not solely as a prelude to fingers and tongues "where it counts," but as a full sexual act in and of itself. Kissing also has symbolic importance to the full range of lesbian sexual activities. The mouth in full view is the tempting sign of the hidden "mouth" a potential partner may discover. And it is an invitation to let you show her what the mouth she sees is going to do to the mouth she conceals.

Kissing the hand   But a kiss should never start mouth to mouth. You are not engaged in the resuscitation of the half-drowned. Like the clitoris, the mouth should wait, blossoming, moistening, preparing for the invading tongue; and the best way to begin is to combine the lips and tongue with that other most sexually assertive portion of a lesbian's body, the hand.

The courtly gesture of a peck on the back of a lady's hand is perhaps a metaphor for the true intentions of the kiss: the hand reversed, the palm can become a veritable theater of sensations, a promise of what these same kisses will bring to the clitoris. Begin with her hand and show, in your kisses, what your hands and mouths and tongues might at last achieve in combination. Let your

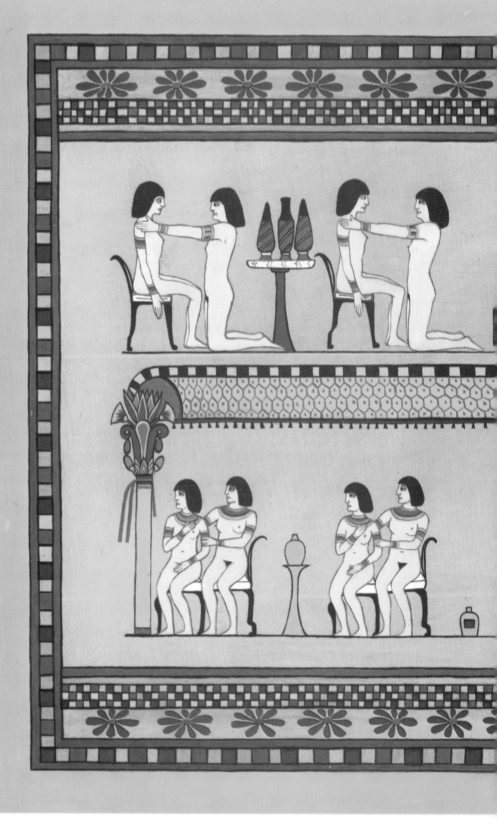

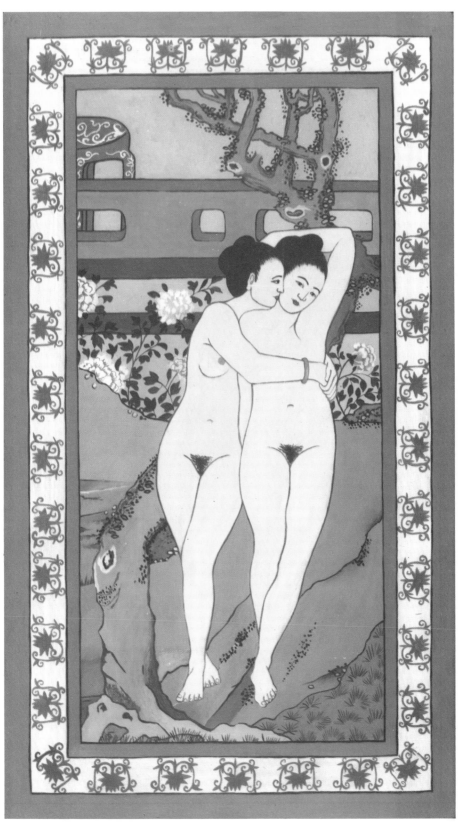

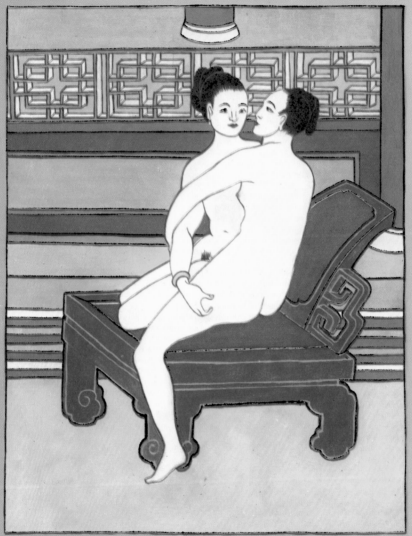

lips bloom at the edge of her palm; as your mouth slightly opens and your tongue curls out, think of a rose unfolding. Make her think of her rose unfolding until all gardens of sight, scent and touch are achieved in the doubling of the two roses. Draw the flesh with gradually increased sucking motions between your teeth; then let your tongue play with the tiny mound of flesh it has captured, until all her body's sensations are fixed in that single place. Then nibble, with the slightest pressure, to the borderline of pain. Then slide your lips toward the heel of the palm and let her live through the kiss as many times as it takes to make a complete circle. But let the most sensitive place—the center—wait for your touch. Deliberately take each finger one by one into your mouth, fluttering your tongue up from root to finger-tip.

You are giving her a choice of two things to think about at this stage. If she is the Girl Next Door or the (former) Sweetheart of Sigma Chi, she may gasp out a memory of butterfly wings in that garden you have made for the two of you. If she's what you hope (even more) she is, her hand will be moving up your thigh, showing to you exactly what she imagines you're doing to her. When you have curled the last finger into your tongue, pause for a moment before introducing her to your final sortie. Then your tongue makes a direct rhythmic hit into her palm's center. Your hand, holding hers, will grasp and release as you gauge and match her response. Don't be surprised if you both discover your free hands living a life of their own during this initial kiss. You may open your eyes to find zippers unzipped, shirts unbuttoned, nipples pinched into attention. And, as always, if the pleasure is matched and mutual, it can be doubled. More certain, however, is your reliance on freedom to choose erotic possibilities. You give, but don't get; you get, but don't give; you both give and get. Stated differently, at any moment the erotic dynamic may flow in new channels. A woman's mouth on the palm of her lover's hand is the literature of all lesbian sexuality.

Kissing the mouth The problem with a lot of mouth-to-mouth kissing is too much too soon. And unfortunately, many lesbians are guilty. Maybe it's another one of those macho notions left over from olden days when lesbians felt they had to emulate male behavior (or, at least, what they assumed was male behavior).

You have met someone new. You barely know her, but you sense there is something there—ideas to exchange, fun to share, maybe love to come, and at any rate you find her attractive, especially around the lips. You approach each other and the next thing you know those lips you had thought looked so sensual have smotheringly clamped over the whole lower half of your face, and out from the gaping maw exposed has sprung a wiggling tongue that darts

for your half-excised tonsils. When you are finally released from her bear-hug grip, gasping for breath and feeling a little like a liter of spit has been dumped into your throat, she looks at you quizzically as if she suspects you of being frigid.

That kind of assault should not be confused with kissing. Nor, we hasten to add, are we criticizing deep tongue kisses. We're merely suggesting that one doesn't start out that way, anymore than (except under very special conditions) a woman would choose to omit all preliminaries and ram something up a lover's vagina.

A kiss or series of kisses—especially at first, whether "at first" means a new lover or the beginning of lovemaking between partners of long standing—begins with a gentle, prolonged exploration of each other's lips. Pulling, gliding, sucking, oscillating, encircling, enfolding—lips parted only slightly, to allow some tentative exploration just inside the lips, against the teeth and gums, against the other's tongue. You can tug a little on different sections of the lip; slide over to peck and gently suck at the very corners where upper and lower lip meet. Vary the intensity just as you vary the pressure of the embrace and where your hands wander; don't be afraid to stop, look at each other and then begin again.

As passion mounts lips part more. Still kissing lips, your tongues gradually slide around each other's. You might suck gently on her tongue, or hold onto it inside your mouth. In-and-out, circling or alternate sucking tongue kisses may please you both, but keep in mind that women differ in their tolerance of or responsiveness to "deep throat" activity. (In fact, it is a good idea to remember that not all women really enjoy deep tongue kissing; if you happen to be among them you are not a freak.)

Since she's probably going to imagine the way you'll kiss "down there" from the way you kiss her mouth, a little restraint may be better than coming off like a clumsy oaf. Once you know each other well, you can risk a little more. In fact, with a woman who really turns you on, you may find yourself enjoying kinds of approaches you thought you didn't like.

A final note: we divided kissing into kissing the hand and kissing the mouth because we believe that both acts of love are especially important to women. We do not, however, suggest that they cannot be intermingled—e.g. darting to the hand after a passionate mouth kiss.

La plume de ma tante Only a feather in fun (as long as it's not from the pet parakeet!) to arouse yourself if you're feeling lazy during a masturbation session or you want to tickle your lover into aroused awakening in the morning. Half-awake yourself, you can, almost without moving, collect your lover's spine into shivers if she is on her side with her back to you, or her inner thighs if she is sprawled on her back or belly, or the crook of her arm or around and about her ear. With a little more effort you can prop yourself on an elbow and wake her with a feather beat against her nipples, her anus or her vulva. Keep a feather apiece on hand for the little theater events you both enact in front of your mirror. The softer and finer your feathers are the better on the whole, but peacock feathers are very good because of their length and iridescence.

Leather   Leather does not play much of a role in lesbian sex. To the large majority of lesbians leather is for clothes—boots, a trenchcoat, or, once you're in the money, skin-tight jean-styled pants. Soaping a saddle is enjoyable and so is inhaling the distinctive scent of new tack, but that's because leather is sensual rather than sexual.

Legal matters   The legal problems that beset committed, productive, responsible individuals who happen to be gay are almost enough to take the joy out of sex. In some ways (for example, in discriminatory tax regulations) they are the same as those faced by all singles, but in others they are compounded several times over.

Our most important advice is to retain a sympathetic and ex-perienced lawyer. You may even find a gay woman or man; they do exist, just as in medicine, theology, academe, psychology–psychia-try, and all the other professions. If your lawyer is not gay, be absolutely certain that she or he knows that you are and that she or he is "sympathetic."

Barring the kind of trouble associated with employment, housing discrimination or even arraignment after the raid of a gay bar (such barbarism does still exist), your legal problems in being a lesbian are apt to fall into four categories. In each situation you need a lawyer:

Custody   With relatively rare exceptions, custody of children automatically used to be granted to the mother in case of divorce. The application of this rule is becoming less and less clear. Straight women are advised to maintain the utmost discretion: that is, don't have affairs with other men while the issue is in dispute. If straight women have problems, they are that much worse for lesbians, who have to be very careful about what's around their homes in the case of some court-appointed social worker's visit. Acknowledging one's lesbian lover or displaying copies of *Christopher Street* (or *The Joy of Lesbian Sex*) on your coffee table might not go over at all well. On the other hand, how does this fit with freeing yourself from decep-tion and coming out of the closet? Not well. Not well at all. Certainly it is time that some healthy, precedent-setting decisions were made by the courts. Help is something that your lawyer is hired for (see also *Lesbian motherhood* and *Coming out*).

Property   Suppose you share an apartment or house with a lover, whose personal property is also there. Suppose you die and well meaning but off-base relatives descend upon the place and take not only "your" piano and dishwasher but also "her" convertible couch and a car she had paid for but for one reason or another registered in your name.

Real Estate   True story: a modest but well cared for and exquisitely furnished country home was shared as a weekend summer retreat by two women who had been lovers for nearly thirty years. The deed was in the name of the slightly older partner, who had years ago bought the property with a small inheritance received before she met the other woman. Suddenly, and regrettably, she died while still in her 50s. Her family ransacked the place of belongings both women had painstakingly acquired over the years and the nephew who acquired the house—in the absence of a proper will— gave his aunt's lover thirty days to vacate so he could establish it as income-producing rental property.

Unless for some reason it is desirable for one of you to have the deed in your name only (in which case you will want to take appropriate steps about who would inherit the real estate), you will probably want to establish joint tenancy.

Your lawyer can arrange this for you as well as telling you how you can get out of such arrangements in the event that the relationship goes sour.

Wills   The law tends to presume that people want to leave their property to spouses and family. So even if a straight person dies intestate, things more often than not end up going to spouse, children or other close relatives.

The law does not recognize the lesbian's lover as her spouse, nor that close circle of warm and beloved friends as family. The only way you can ensure that your property is distributed as you wish is to draw up a formal will with everything clearly spelled out. Do *not* be tempted to try this on your own. Home-made wills are questionable enough to begin with (and rarely honored), and even in this age of increasing enlightenment gay rights is a concept still frequently associated with radical extremism.

Be certain that a competent lawyer prepares your will. Some lesbians and gay men are including various gay-rights causes as beneficiaries; you may wish to consider this, too. If you do not have the financial resources to hire a personal lawyer you will find that free or very-low-cost legal assistance can be obtained in most major cities and in the county seats of most rural areas. Catalogs listing resources available to women may also be of help. If you feel you do not own enough to bother with making a will remember that by making a clear disposition of your possessions you prevent unpleasant wrangles and that through your will you can make simple gifts, however small, to friends. You don't have to leave them a fortune.

Legs and thighs Legs are enormously sensitive to extragenital sex acts. You can try cupping a hand under your lover's slightly bent knee as you stroke her entire leg with your other hand, your fingernails, feather-like objects, or your tongue and lips. Gentle but insistent movements against her inner

thigh rapidly accelerate the action. Another supersensitive area is where thigh and torso meet. Ditto where ass and thigh meet. No area —wherever it may be—that your attention evokes response (for example, some women react to having the flesh right above their knee pinched; or the hollow behind the knee) should be neglected.

As to shaving or not shaving, we'll capsulize what we said under *Armpits*. Make your choice according to what seems right for you (and your lover) rather than as a response to fad. Some women find not shaving "liberating" and more natural. Some women find it unesthetic and somehow "masculine." If you shave and she doesn't (or vice versa) and the difference is in any way bothersome to either of you, talk it over in a cooperative, negotiating spirit; it is often seeming trivia that grow into problems that turn people off.

A thigh can be grasped between your legs and rubbed on until you come (for some women, this will be a "small" orgasm; for others— many favor the technique—fully satisfying). Thighs can be encircled as you dance, providing hints of passion to come. They can be slapped playfully, though some women consider it macho-butch and are definitely annoyed, or they can be squeezed together for some look-no-hands masturbation when the mood strikes you.

Possibly one of the best things about thighs—inner thighs, that is—is their tremendous responsiveness to slow, light, but ardent stroking. Starting at knee level you gradually work your way up to where they join your lover's torso. Don't be hasty about sliding into her crotch. If her inner thighs are hairy (and many women's are, it is definitely *not* freaky) use the very tips of your fingers to circle about that hair.

Many women are excited by a light rubbing against the thighs with breasts or hair (even if it's short). Flutter them with your eyelids; when you kiss, suck and tongue them, always go slowly. To prolong the pleasure, yours and hers, don't be too quick to move to her vulva. Instead, slide your mouth and hands up over her hip bone and to the navel, back down over her pubic hair and back again to her thighs before going between her legs.

Lesbian motherhood The traditional view: children are the natural, hoped-for, *blessed* product of a union between two people who love each other and are prepared to share that love in the context of family life.

The reality: if the above were always true, the offices of shrinks would not be filled with men, women and children for whom that scheme of things has somehow gone awry, either now or a generation ago. And those who seek help from psychotherapy do not, of course, include the many who turn to religious counseling, the many who seek escape in drink or drugs, or those who pick up a gun to end it all either for themselves or someone close to them. Police records show that most murders happen in the context of "normal" family life. And then there are the great hordes who simply grin and bear it.

But tradition is a hard nut to crack, especially when the hammer is your reality and the tradition has the unqualified sanction of the entire Judaeo-Christian culture. Whether one is a "believer" in that culture or not, its influence pervades every corner of our lives and it is difficult—though not impossible—intelligently to escape it. Its power ranges from the bedroom, influencing choice—even method—of birth control, to a woman's decision about what will, or will not, happen inside her own body.

To the power of religious belief is added a whole network of societal dicta, a network that has, for many, taken on the hue of a conspiracy. Keeping women "barefoot and pregnant" and consequently tied to the home leaves men free to get out and do all the interesting work, secure in the belief that their little heirs are being raised to follow honorably in their footsteps.

But a "conspiracy" implies conscious planning, and we frankly doubt that much thought was ever given to the Blessed Product arrangement—as is the case with most human situations that don't, any longer, work well for most people. Usually what passes for thought on the matter consists of some vague conviction that what was still is and therefore always should be, despite the obvious drawbacks.

So, for whatever combination of religious, cultural and socio-economic reasons one might cite (and they are infinite), hetero-sexual marriage, its manufacture of at least 2.3 Blessed Products, and its leech-like hold on traditional forms of family life still constitute our treasured norm.

The fact that an alarming number of such alliances either go up in smoke or grimly continue in emotional pain for all concerned has not escaped the notice of societal overseers. But, again, the facts of the matter have made few inroads on the traditional view and its definitions of what is necessary for happiness, sanity, and health in human life.

Freeing oneself from the tentacles of the traditional view results in the realization that there *are* alternatives, that there *is* such a thing as freedom of choice. One of the most dramatic disclosures of this freeing process is frequently a changed view of who children are, what they are and how we might, as adults, relate differently to them.

Though many have been tried, there is still no alternative that obviates the awesome responsibilities in raising children for seventeen to twenty years of your life. The financial aspects alone of parenthood demand a relentless stability; the old expression that having children is giving hostages to fortune still holds immense emotional truth: in the long journey through dirty diapers by the dozen, through the shards of your only real porcelain vase, through the terrors and miseries of chicken pox and broken arms, the right schools and wrong schools, parent survival and child survival are remorselessly interdependent. If the darlings pull your purse strings hard, they yank the heart strings even harder. And as if this were not enough,the mother also carries the burden of knowledge that it is she who is the child's first love object; that on the memory of that first love the child will base all other interpersonal relationships and learn the meaning of intimacy.

Still, women do it: some *crave* doing it. No argument yet devised has put an effective stop to the yearning of women to give all or a part of themselves to motherhood. The joy, it seems, outweighs the terror.

So if women generally still want children, where does this leave lesbian women? Given the right attitude and approach—in a very good place. Whether she has had her children as a result of a previous heterosexual life, or whether as a lesbian she chooses to have children, the lesbian is perhaps freer than the rest of humankind of the old baggage of the Blessed Product myth. Particularly in the case of the latter group, lesbians do not base their decisions to have and raise a child on any thoughtless compulsion to conform to the female role. Rather, lesbians are motivated to be mothers from a desire to provide love, care and support for a new human being and to share the pleasure they find in their own company with another. Lesbians have children. Lesbians do not make extensions of themselves or of a family name.

Women in both tradition and fact tend to be gentle, tender, given to cuddling, yet they are curiously adept at the use of firm discipline in non-punitive ways. Barring hang-ups that either block or have warped these qualities' development, women make the best parents. Freed from the role-playing of straight family life, lesbians have the capacity to make ideal mothers.

Hence, there is no inherent barrier to a lesbian having a child or children just because she is a lesbian. An increasing number of women are exercising their freedom of choice *not* to have children, basically because they are beginning to understand that the possession of a womb is not necessarily synonymous with being a good mother, but if you decide, as a lesbian, that you also have it in you to be a good mother, there may be problems aside from the usual ones of diapers, chicken pox and schools. Usually these problems are no more than those attendant on any child's discovery that her or his family is "different" (see *Children of lesbians*)—that they are Jewish in a WASP community, or Catholic in a Protestant community, or adopted, or poorer, or that their mother has a tin ear and Jodie's can sing *Traviata*.

When the problems are more serious, even ugly, the cause is usually coming from an overwhelming amount of heterosexist influence on the child, pressuring her or him to despise what the surrounding society despises. This situation, however, even when it is extreme, can often be nipped in the bud if the child has been treated to the facts, as well as to love, at home. Lesbians, perhaps even more than straight parents, must consistently level with their children. Honesty from you is as important as security. One little girl who at the age of six rose up in her pink party dress and bashed a bigger boy's nose in because he called her mother a "dirty queer" now, as a teenager, moves with wonderful ease in both straight and gay circles and everywhere is both loved and loving, intelligent and strong. Unfortunately for those of you who long for rural life, the mother of this child credits much of her successful development to exposing her, from infancy, to lesbian friends, associates and events in and out of the home so that the child knew, at the gut level, that her mother—and her mother's lover—were not unique, i.e. were not "aberrations." Urban areas still are the places where the most lesbians gather, and where they are most sociable and open with one another.

Some problems (such as legal complications, difficulties obtaining loan or mortgage money, nearly total responsibility if there is no partner involved) resemble those suffered by any single parent. What, for example, about your social life? Your friends phone at the last minute to urge you to join them at the local watering-hole-cum-dance-floor, but how do you find a sitter (or iron a shirt or take a shower and also feed/read to little Mona or little Murray) in less than half an hour? Or you do manage an evening out and that stranger across the crowded bar turns out to be love's young dream. Is it your place, where the twins have probably let the hamsters loose in your pillow cases, or hers? So you wind up by dawn's early light facing your sitter (and her bill for $50.97) while reeking of sex and Tequila Sunrises.

But then, maybe it's worse if you're not single. It's hard to act out your little *plume de ma tante* fantasy to wake your lover in the morning when you're steeled to hear the baby scream; or let yourself go for more than just a quick hump through faded denim against the kitchen counter when the entire little league may roar through for peanut butter at any minute. If straight mothers know that motherhood is no joke, then lesbian mothers know it in triplicate.

Also, the children of heterosexuals usually learn that Daddy has at least as much right to Mommy (or vice versa) as they do, and emotional trade-offs are organized because both adults and kids understand the legal and socially accepted right of access. But the children and lover of the lesbian mother can enact fierce wars over the issue of who's-getting-the-most-of-mom and, unless the situation is openly confronted and discussed, without apology or defensiveness on any side, the children will almost always win. And what have they won? A mother alone again, slightly more embittered toward the little darlings she just sacrificed her sex life to.

Some problems concern what, when, and how to tell the child or children: how to deal with the heterosexism that bombards its way into the kindergarten cloakroom or sails across the airwaves of most TV programs (see *Children of lesbians*).

Difficulties can also cluster around more minor but potentially explosive aspects of lesbian motherhood. The mother may begin to re-question her sexual identity, almost involuntarily wishing for a straight life to accord with her "straight" role as a mother. Her partner, if there is one, may begin to experience untoward jealousy and may decide—faced with the reality of children underfoot all day long—that the whole thing was somebody else's idea, certainly not hers. Such a situation is not unlike that often experienced by husbands after the arrival of a child, when midnight candlelit dinners give way to 4 a.m. feedings. Even the most responsible and willing of partners may expect this emotional crisis, but success for everyone depends on working it through with reassurances of better times to come all round, not on running like hell.

The baby-altered situation may also create a pull toward aping family life and abandoning lesbian reality. These impulses should be recognized for what they are, especially if you're intent on raising a human being, not a Blessed Product.

None of these problems is insoluble and the last mentioned are as amenable to psychotherapeutic help (if needed) as are similar ones that arise in straight relationships.

The point is that no woman need deny herself the privilege of raising a child just because she is a lesbian. But she should definitely *not* have a child just because she is a woman.

Some lesbian mothers marry and have a child (or two) before they have made the decision to come out. Given a vindictive husband, custody problems can have heartbreaking, as well as expensive, results. The problem usually arises when the father (almost always after he's re-married) suddenly wonders at the "fitness" of a lesbian raising his (*sic*) child. We are glad to report that many of these cases are now receiving excellent media coverage, with the positive results of the public's re-evaluating their notions of lesbianism and motherhood. Fortunately, a great many marriages are dissolved tearlessly (often because the father, too, was basically gay without knowing it) with the mother getting custody of the children and the father generous visiting rights.

So the following is addressed to lesbians who are fully in touch with their gayness and who are contemplating having and/or raising children. Even then, a great deal of discussion and tremendous mutuality of agreement should precede any final decision.

If you are with a loving partner, what is her feeling about the whole matter? How do the two of you propose to raise the child in the context of your own special relationship versus the cultural mores of "Family Life"?

If you are not with a partner, do you feel that your having a child might have an effect (deleterious or otherwise) on some future relationship?

How do you, a lesbian, propose to get pregnant and is your lover in agreement with your plan? Some women will have no problem at all in acceding to their lover's sleeping with some appropriate and accommodating male (in some cases a gay or bisexual man both partners like and respect but who will have no second thoughts on his "rights" of fatherhood later on. If the two of you want the baby to be solely yours, you will not want, for example, the man to be named on the birth certificate.) If you choose this method, careful watching of the ovulation clock may result in pregnancy with only one encounter with the male in question. But the partners of some lesbians may find even one time a mind-blowing threat and the image of the beloved in bed with a man may linger to erode the relationship. Because of this, some lesbians prefer the more impersonal approach of using a sperm bank. A few women have expressed interest in being personally involved in injecting the fluid into their lovers, but more react to this as too kinky an idea.

Have you considered adoption? A great many gay women who want to have children want to *have* them—that is, experience pregnancy and delivery. Other women are less interested in the biological and psychological features of pregnancy. Indeed, many of them (straight women included) would just as soon not be bothered. For many women who want a child, adoption may be a successful answer. Between partners, the mutuality of adoption (two agreeing to take and raise, rather than one bearing) may be healthier for particular relationships. Adoption by "single" parents (even those who are publicly gay) is on the increase, though hardly, especially if you live in Middle America, commonplace. Because of their own civil rights battles, gay people are, on the whole, strikingly less prejudiced than straights. Thus a baby of a different race might, for gays, be even more special than one of their own. The less specific you are in your requirements (for example, *not* white, *not* under six months, *not* of WASP stock) the easier it may be to get a child.

Once you have a child, what do you do with it?

Probably just what you imagined: you love it, care for it, teach it, help it to grow, protect it but let it go free. You introduce it to all the things meaningful to you personally, not those meaningful to straight society. If this means Mozart and snowball fights and a gay Thanksgiving dinner for fifteen instead of Disneyland, then all the better. Your child stands perhaps a better chance than most to grow into a caring, loving, well-integrated person because he or she was never swaddled in the myth of the Blessed Product. And, as a lesbian, you are in an excellent position to appreciate the wounds of bias and bigotry. Thus your child has a good chance to grow up accepting people as people, and will have the chance to learn earlier than most the absurdity of categories.

If your child is a boy, expect to get some flack about how he's going to miss out on "male identification." Your best answer to this may be to let everybody know that you believe manhood is best defined as personhood; and let your son know that too.

If your child is a girl, expect to get some flack about how tough it's going to be when she turns adolescent and you (or your lover) will get the hots for her. Of all the ugly myths surrounding gay women, this is the most distasteful and erroneous. It's ironic that the same myth is not applied to the straight mothers of young sons. And, you may recall, Humbert Humbert was *not* a woman.

A summarizing note of caution: you shouldn't go out and have and/or raise a child just because lesbians are also entitled, but have a child only if it is *entirely* O.K. for both you and your partner. And if you feel quite certain it will be entirely O.K. for the child too.

And—need we add?—do *not* feel guilty or "unwomanly" if you don't want anybody under twenty sharing your life and bathtowels.

Lesbos   The Greek island from which the word lesbianism is derived. In the sixth century B.C. the home of Sappho, who educated the young women at her school in the delights of the body as well as the life of the mind. Her surviving poetry sings of love and the loss of love; passion and the death of passion. While Lesbos today is a far cry from the place Sappho made famous, it still has significance as the spiritual home of today's lesbians, a promised land of the lesbian imagination.

Little death   The swoon of orgasm featured as "the little death" of early English lyrics, "*la petite mort*" of French poetry. Sometimes the effect is so profound that the little death is total, if momentary, unconsciousness. It's well to advise your partner ahead of time if orgasm knocks you cold, or you may, if she is of a practical nature, wake up in a hospital emergency room.

Little theater Once you thoroughly understand that there is no other purpose to lesbian sexuality than pleasure (*not* acquiring a matched set of silver bonbon dishes; *not* your little bit toward the birth control movement) then you can invent endless variations on the theme of pleasure and let yourself have time to play. We mean play in the sense that children enjoy play—engaged in intensely, with passion and purpose; play that blots out the world of ordinary concerns and creates a special world out of the imagination. Little theater is exactly that kind of play, and is most productively engaged in by long-time lovers who have shared their dreams and fantasies as well as their sex lives—again, like children who are "best friends" and can wordlessly pick up on a game that had to be abandoned the evening before, each knowing exactly what the other's roles and expectations are.

Little theater is little indeed: a performance of, and for, two alone; no audience required. Performance alone can be its object, or performance can be used as a bridge to particular kinds of sexual activity the performance excites. It can happen in the nude, in ordinary street clothes or it can involve a whole theatrical wardrobe, including makeup, wigs and costume jewelry. Most lesbians who play little theater also invest in a wide full-length mirror—a place to watch themselves and admire themselves becoming another character. The dialogue is, of course, invented on the spot. The character each lesbian plays may be whoever and whatever she has always (or just recently) wanted to be, shifting through historical epochs if necessary, bridging time and space as required: if Queen Christina of Sweden wants to meet Queen Elizabeth I for an evening's tryst, so be it. If Joan of Arc wants to seduce Madame Bovary, so be it. Sometimes little theater has a wild comic streak to it—such as the kind brought about when two entirely hip and sophisticated New York City lesbians decide to act out the renunciation scene between Stephen Gordon and sweet little Mary in Radclyffe Hall's *The Well of Loneliness*, one playing the martyred butch calling on God for the salvation of queers, the other beating the breast that covers the broken heart. It is likely that the performance concluded with these same highly liberated role-rejecting New Yorkers in bed playing butch and femme there too, just as Stephen and Mary did and just for further kicks. Sometimes little theater exposes real sexual fantasies, such as wondering what it would be like to be fucked by a Mysterious Intruder after she's chased you around the house, finally captured you and tied you up; or supposing your lover has become a vampire in a long black cape swirling over your hypnotized (and negligently clad) form to suck the pulse from your throat. One of the most sexually thrilling acts for a little theater performance consists of little more than (in front of your mirror)

dressing your lover up in the costume of your choice and then, standing behind her so that both of you can watch, slowly and deliberately peeling it all off again, piece by piece.

Lesbians, as long as they let their imaginations take control of their fantasy life and stop living by the societally built-in heterosexual guidebook, are the most inventive and playful creatures in the world. Little theater allows you to sharpen your lesbian imagination and, further, teaches you more about your sexual self.

Loneliness The best advice we can offer lesbians who complain of loneliness is to stop seeking its cure in love and romance. Begin to value friendship as much as you have learned to value love. Find your local women's center and check out the lesbian activities it sponsors. Write to "Lesbian Connection" (see our Bibliography): describe your situation and ask for contacts in your area. Write to the National Gay Task Force (again check the Bibliography) for their directory of gay and lesbian–feminist organizations (there are more than a thousand). In urban areas, there is frequently a Lesbian Switchboard (listed in the phone book) to refer you to events organized locally by lesbians and to lesbian meeting places.

Love To state the obvious: it can't be taught. Love is an emotion that is either there or it's not and while sex can be "done" love must be *felt* before it can be *made*—made in the sense of a creative rather than a mechanical activity. Certainly we believe that the best sex happens between women who are truly lovers, not just sex partners, but for lesbians to become lovers, for them to maintain and nurture their love, there are special problems.

Western culture has popularly expressed heterosexual love through publicity: we are all familiar with new man–woman lovers dancing on the ceiling, singing in the rain, necking in the sunlight— and eventually inviting all the friends and relatives to gather around to bless their love with sets of kitchenware and silver candle- sticks. There are photographs in the newspapers; church and state applaud. Even "illicit" heterosexual love can have some kind of recognition: blurred copies of Romeo and Juliet are as common, at every level of the culture, as brands of detergent (and all the "same but different" as Gertrude Stein sardonically remarked).

A lesbian falls in love just like anybody else; she can't sleep, she can't eat, she walks on air; she would rather be on a lumpy mattress with her beloved than on the throne of the Romanovs. The great difference (and damage) for her is in the area of public expression. Lovers need to shout it from the rooftops. Most heterosexuals can, and be forgiven by dewy-eyed neighbors for disturbing the peace: most lesbians can't. While it is heartening to see young lesbians holding hands in the street or kissing in the parks it is likely that their public display of love is based more on defiance and bravado than on the simple spilling-over of emotion. Even this limited show of feeling is still very much a phenomenon of sophisticated cities, and even there it is tolerated only in certain gay parts of town. The liberation of lesbian love in, for instance, Twin Stumps, Idaho, or Crooked Foot, North Carolina, is likely, at best, to be greeted with sniggers, jeers and insults—at worst, with being put in the local

asylum. The association of lesbian love with "wells," "pits," "shadows," "loneliness," "torment," "hells" and "outcasts" is based on a largely correct assessment of social reality—and not as much on cowardice as the naive might think. Lesbian love must remain guarded, must learn invisibility, must walk a tightrope of caution in most places, or else fear for its life. But the irreducible character of love demands publicity as well as privacy. What, in effect, is the "life" of any kind of love without the freedom to declare itself to the cop on the beat as well as to mom and dad?

We think it grows sick with fear; that it collects guilt and neurosis the way ailing plants collect bugs; that it turns in on itself and begins to believe in its bad reputation instead of in the joy that created it. We also think that the best cure for a lesbian love that is being poisoned at its erotic source is to start getting mad at the poisoner, not at the lover. It's a very good idea to have some kind of gay community in which love can be openly expressed without fear of challenge, and if your part of the country can't give you that community do everything in your power to get yourself to a place that can. Finally, stop thinking heterosexual. Understand that your love and your lovemaking is not like anything else on earth, that it is a unique and fabulous manifestation of Eros that's been around since the beginning of the human race in every time, place and culture. Understand that beyond ordinary and intelligent standards of discretion and responsibility, you create a lesbian reality that is just as purposeful, useful and love-enhancing as anyone's. You don't have to feel cheated because you can't have a wedding with organ music in the same church where your parents were married. Understand that heterosexual ceremonies and rituals around love are meant to reflect heterosexual erotic reality, not yours. If you yearn for ceremony, make your own, based on the joy that's authentically lesbian. Just keep in mind that oppression coupled with a consciousness of oppression has historically made people stronger. If discretion and responsibility and care are required to keep your lesbian love alive, *belief* in that love as a genuine and healthy human reality is essential to its delight. No one can promise you an immediate future of shouting from the rooftops, but these suggestions may take your love out of the shadows: most importantly, out of the shadows your own mind makes.

Lubrication Some lesbians complain of too much wetness rather than too little. If this becomes a problem in oral sex (which doesn't mean there's something "wrong" with you), the vaginal insertion of a dildo or some fingers can make you more comfortable in pursuing clitoral mouthwork. If you're both secure enough to believe it won't be taken as a rejection, gently wipe her with a clean cloth. While we're on the subject, some women with sensitive skin will need to wash afterwards; this does not mean there is anything "wrong" with either of you, any more than too much lubrication does.

If dryness is a problem, saliva will usually correct the situation. Or you may want to keep a tube of sterile jelly handy (this is especially useful if you're using dildos, and is very close to mandatory if you are planning on anal penetration). Petroleum jelly is greasy, and tends to taste like you're swimming in an oil spill. If you are going to experiment with yummy foods or thick liqueurs, have some towels around and, again, don't take it amiss if your lover runs to the bathroom to wash off the stickiness.

Marriage Marriage was invented in the first place to provide safe breeding grounds and to protect economic assets through inheritance. Neither reason applies to long-term lesbian relationships. Whether lesbians "believe" in marriage, ideologically or simply as an appropriate acknowledgement of love between two people, there's no escaping the effects of this heterosexual institution on lesbian style and habits. All discussion of fidelity and of monogamy versus non-monogamy, all romantic conflict involving perceptions of sexual jealousy, possessiveness, betrayal or promiscuity and all economic and legal problems (e.g. taxation status and child custody) either directly or indirectly reflect the monolithic presence of the concept of marriage in our society. For many lesbians, to discuss marriage and lesbianism in the same breath is to define an anomaly. Lesbianism, ideally, is an impulse toward erotic freedom; marriage, traditionally, is an end to it—a fact that heterosexuals too are beginning to realize and resist.

Lesbians, increasingly conscious of the positive differences between themselves and heterosexuals, reject more and more the model of marriage as the pattern for their relationships, but they still tend to look for a primary partner, a primary relationship in which intimacy, personality and friendship, as well as sexuality, can be savored over a long period of time (see *Fidelity*). Such relationships also provide a bulwark against loneliness and a sense of social definition in a society which still, by and large, recognizes the couple as its essential human unit. But very few lesbians any longer refer to such a relationship as a marriage. In rejecting the word, they are rejecting the limitations of the concept; they are, instead, finding ways to reinforce erotic essence and liberty. Crucial to this change in thinking and behavior is the recognition that sexual engagement with a stranger or a friend does not indicate promiscuity or disloyalty to the prime lover—that, indeed, sexual pleasure on the outside can bring stimulation and renewal to sex on the home front.

Also on the increase is the lesbian who totally rejects domestication of love, who is a loner and is proud of it; typically she is young and sees her lesbianism as an image of freedom, an explicit expression of the power to get and have anything and anyone she wishes, and of the strength of reliance on self-love. "Loneliness" is a condition she reverses into a creative time for self-exploration, for friendships, for heady adventure-seeking and for serious work free from romantic distraction. She does not necessarily cruise or deliberately set out to pick up somebody for a one-night stand. But her success in sexual adventuring is in direct proportion to her belief in herself.

Much of this new self-image in lesbians has been nurtured through feminism and through the radical lesbian political ideology which defines heterosexism and its institutional frameworks (especially that of marriage) as a system based on the oppression of all women and on male domination of women. To reject man sexually, therefore, is to reject all the systems meant to repress the sexual (and therefore the creative) potential of the female. But for those lesbians who view such a position as outright folly or who feel it requires an excess of courage, both traditional and modified forms of marriage still make sense. These lesbians still seek partners with whom they can imagine a life-long process of living and working together, maintaining complete sexual fidelity. As in most straight marriages, however, the prohibitions implicit in such an arrangement usually result in eventual sexual death: the couple may grow old together, enjoying each other's company while paying off the mortgage, but the elements of mystery, fantasy and curiosity most people still need for sexual stimulation, once satisfied, are seldom renewable. But it is difficult for women, even lesbians, to pull out overnight from the centuries of brainwashing which inextricably associate (for women) sex with marriage. To perceive the injustice of the sexual double-standard intellectually is one thing; to get the body and the imagination to deal with the erotic facts in a social context is quite another.

For lesbians engaged in this struggle (and most are) we return again to the concept of negotiation, and recommend courage in discussion, if not in behavior, of erotic reality. While it is not unheard of for lesbians to embrace the heterosexual notion of traditional marriage, including role-playing, wedding ceremonies in gay churches (with flowers, satin and singing), vows of love eternal and even actual reference to each other as "husband" and "wife," such instances are and have always been extremely rare. Even before the liberating effects of feminism on lesbian self-image and style, few lesbian couples saw themselves as mirror images of traditional heterosexual bonding. Most lesbians seeking a lasting relationship

still fall between the two extremes of behavior described here, "marriage" and total independence, wishing for stability and sexual fidelity, organizing their lives around a domestic arrangement together. These women, too, however, are more and more engaged in a struggle to integrate a more libertarian approach to sexual gratification into their relationships and, in doing so, find themselves constantly assessing the origins of monogamous concepts, constantly battling against what they regard as societally-induced feelings of sexual betrayal and guilt when they step outside the relationship for sex. Such lesbians walk an emotional tightrope between adventure and intimacy and are, to their pleased astonishment, realizing that the effort is often worth it: they are having their cake and eating it too.

Married lesbians Reversing the gender referred to in a chant popular in Gay Liberation marches of the mid-1970s: "2-4-6-8, How do you know your wife is straight?"

Surveys, the declarations of married lesbians and experience in clinical practice (psychotherapy, psychoanalysis, and information gathered in other branches of medicine—gynecology in particular) all suggest that a surprising proportion of married women are "really" lesbians. That is, their greatest emotional pull is toward other women; they enjoy and seek out the company of women; they frequently have one "special friend" with whom the bond of caring and communication surpasses that which they can reach with a man; they are physically attracted to other women; and—not always, but we believe far oftener than is generally recognized—they sexualize a relationship with a woman (or women).

Why then do they remain at least ostensibly straight? Well, on the practical level (some people might call it a negative level) it is not always easy for women to come out, let alone come out of the closet, despite some inroads carved by Gay Liberation. This is especially true in areas where there is not ready access to a visible gay community, and in areas where the social mores remain Victorian or worse. It is also the case when there are deeply felt external pressures (e.g. family) or deeply felt internal pressures (e.g. her own family) that cause a woman to choose to remain within the straight fold despite her sexual and affectional preference. But there can be other reasons, too. Some women are genuinely capable of loving and making love with members of either sex (see *Bisexuality*); although sometimes this is a cop-out for not coming out as gay, this is by no means always the case. As supporters of self-determination and people's right to live as they choose, we believe that this stance is perfectly O.K. when a woman is committed to it.

There are, of course, other married lesbians who are avowedly lesbians but who—again, for reasons that are perfectly valid for them—still wish to stay married. Often, but not always, the husband is a gay man with similar needs. We've known some of these marriages to be characterized by considerable warmth and affection, sometimes with a child or two who grow up in an atmosphere of tolerance and wiseness that may be hard to duplicate in strictly straight families. Again, practical considerations may play a role: tax benefits, hospitalization-plan benefits, greater mobility in living quarters, avoiding social stigma. We deplore the fact that society is still structured so as to make these factors viable in adults' choice of living schemes, but it is definitely not *people* who are to be deplored. In short, it's the system that deserves censure and requires change not the gay women (and men) who are trapped within it.

A number of married lesbians manage to keep their real love lives from interfering with their marriages. But it's not without pitfalls: for example, lover or husband might fall prey to the green-eyed monster, jealousy, or the juggling of who's-on-for-tonight can prove too stressful for the woman herself. Given mutual caring, a mature outlook on the process of negotiating, and shared faith in such a life-style, all parties concerned may be able to work through the problems. If not, some counseling with a psychotherapist sympathetic to such problems and experienced in dealing with them may be of help.

Massage   One of the more notable contributions massage parlors have made to our current life-styles has been popularizing the connection between massage and sex. Since every inch of your skin is a part of one big sense organ, it's only natural that being massaged can be experienced as having sex, extragenitally. It's also lovemaking of the most flattering order, as it suggests that you are touchable everywhere.

Straddling your lover or crouching beside her is mostly a matter of your separate anatomies. Mutual comfort is the touchstone, because a good massage takes time. It should never be hurried, and it should not be cut off with two firm presses to the *latissimus dorsi* because you're too tired to do more. If that's the situation, save the whole procedure for a stronger moment.

Your partner should lie flat on her belly, without a pillow under her head. (She can turn her head from side to side, which will switch the prominence of certain muscles and give you a chance to work on the side of the neck previously hidden.) Some women can lie with their heads straight down, with most of the weight on the forehead to allow for breathing, or two pillows can be spaced closely together with just enough room for the nose to fit between. (Pillows will, however, accentuate the curve of the neck.)

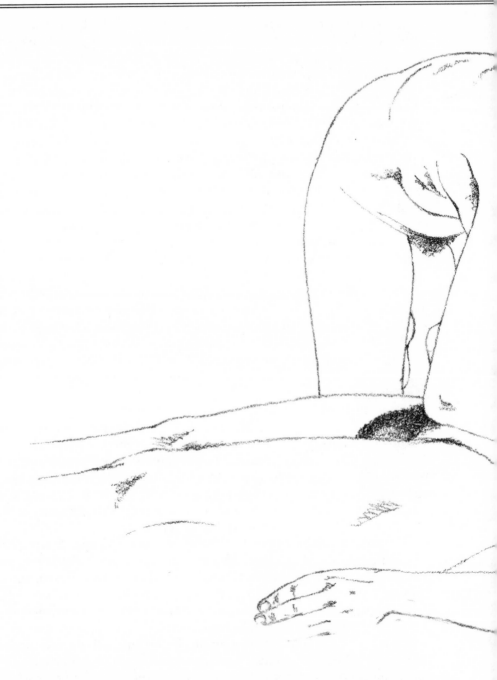

Start with the neck, using all four fingers as a broad surface to stroke rather heavily down from behind the ear to the shoulder and out. Again, take your time and move slowly. Clasp both hands at the base of the neck, so that your fingers touch her clavicles and your two thumbs can press deeply (around and around) near that

big bump which is, in most people, the seventh cervical vertebra. After a while your hands move out, over and around the shoulder and then across the top of the back between the outer shoulder and spinal column.

It helps to study charts of back muscles, to know where they start, where they end, and how they work and stretch in between. At the very least, study your lover's back very carefully and experiment with your motions, the direction of the rub and the amount of pressure.

Work your way down as slowly as you can. Many women respond to fairly strong, concentrated pressure with the thumbs at both sides of the spinal column while the palms and fingers fan outward, finally moving all the way out to her sides. When you get to her lower back, a good amount of palm pressure can be used against the pelvic bones; keep your palms in two symmetrical places and rotate in a small, vibrating kind of motion. With your thumbs (or fingers) go all the way down along the sides of her tailbone until it disappears in the crack between her buttocks.

There are countless variations to the back-rub massage, but one of the most delightful is to lie flat on the floor, face up. Crouching or straddling above your head, your lover then reaches under your back as far as she can and, using considerable finger pressure, comes all the way up your back (along the spinal column) and up the back of your neck, which she can cradle against the front of her thighs. This produces a real feeling of stretching, very close to mild traction on a flat surface. One caution: be careful about the kind of rug or flooring; the heavier the partner the greater the chance of the massager's sustaining knuckle burns.

Since all skin is massageable one should not stop with backs. Feet are a favorite, and you and your lover may want to try lying foot-to-head and give each other simultaneous foot massages. With your fingers clasping her instep, try pressing your thumbs against the soles in one slow, gliding motion from heel to toes. Knead the ball of the foot and gently move each toe in circular motions. Arms and hands deserve massaging, too.

Needless to say, fronts should not be neglected in favor of backs. But whereas the back can stand an enormous amount of pressure and "digging" (in fact, ineffectual back rubbers are people who go too lightly), the front is more for soft stroking—fingertips, fingernails gently applied, lips and tongues. The same goes for the face—eyelids, nose, cheeks—although both the cheek bones and the forehead (try this the next time one of you has a headache) can stand a lot more pressure; ditto the head.

While a good body massage can stimulate you both right into genital lovemaking, it can also be so rewardingly relaxing that sleep is in order. Be sure you have a consensus on this, or you may get all revved up only to see your lover slip into blissful sleep, from which she won't want to be awakened, even for lovemaking.

As for lotions, use them or don't use them, as you prefer. It's a matter of choice, not of right or wrong.

Mastectomy   As we said under *Hysterectomy and oophorectomy*, neither the uterus nor the ovary is an anatomical site of lovemaking. Alas, the breast is. Thus both the psychological and physical implications of breast removal are apt to be more profound than those of the other two operations.

Should you or your lover be faced with the necessity for mastectomy, it is essential that you discuss openly your feelings, your fears, your fantasies about how it may affect each of you and your relationship. Most lesbians are fully in touch with how much pleasure they derive from breast-play in lovemaking, both as recipients and givers, so there is no use in denying that something will be missing. The loss needs to be felt and grieved. While a good prosthesis takes care of appearances in most circumstances (including wearing bikinis), in bed the loss will be obvious.

Don't be too quick to protest that it won't matter. Chances are that, eventually, given a mature and loving relationship, it won't. But don't rush to give assurances too prematurely. They won't be believed, and you'll end up doubting how much you meant it.

Demand as much information as you can get about the extent of the operation, how the area will look afterwards (try to get a drawing or, better yet, some photographs of women who have had the same procedure), etc. Discuss all this with your lover. Cooperate in preparing each other.

Try to make contact with other women who have had mastectomies (most major hospitals can be of help here) and especially with lesbians. People who have been in the same boat are usually quite adept at throwing lifelines. Again, share these experiences with your lover.

Since sheer sex is not at the very heart of most lesbian relationships, it is good to spend some time focusing on the things other than sex that you both treasure in your relationship. But don't pretend for a moment that a quick burst of positive thinking will eliminate your anxieties. It just doesn't work like that, but with patience and caring you both will most likely adapt successfully.

So far we have spoken of the lesbian facing mastectomy but who has a lover's support. How about the unattached gay woman?

For her the operation will be just as traumatic, and therefore all the advice to settled couples (except, obviously, the discussions with her lover) applies. But although lacking the support of someone very special in a time of enormous travail, she may in one very important area have an easier time of it. Many relationships are damaged when one of the partners changes, but once a woman is breastless a new lover is likely to accept her state from the outset. It is perhaps a poor consolation, but it does mean that her life can continue much as before.

Masturbation Women have always masturbated, but somehow the humorous saying "Let's not and say we did," got reversed to "Let's do it and say we didn't." No female collegian of the 1950s or earlier 1960s could have failed to wonder why, when she found masturbation nerve-zappingly delicious, so few of her sorority sisters "did it." Well, they lied. (The other saying goes: "ninety-nine in one hundred do it and say so; the other one is lying.")

Skill at masturbating brings extra rewards for lesbians because lovemaking by hand plays a prominent role in their sexual repertoire. What feels good to you, teases and excites you, primes you for climax and then leaves you throbbing in whirlpools of post-orgasm delight is pretty much what will work for her, too.

However, lovemaking between two people is not masturbation, even though the actual techniques may be similar. Masturbation means *self*-stimulation, and, quite apart from the healthy effects of a good orgasm or two, it can be a tremendously liberating experience. If your lover is away for a month and you don't feel like making it with someone else, or if you don't have a lover to begin with, or you feel like having sex and she doesn't, or simply that you want to expand upon the sexual activities you share, masturbation is the happy solution—although, we hasten to add, you don't need a specific "problem": just wanting to masturbate is a perfectly good reason for doing it. And, minus lover or otherwise not getting enough, it's the only way to keep yourself in shape—that is, to avoid premature sexual senility.

Let's not start with the obvious. That is, since the clitoris is what makes it all work, it's best not to attack it with a vengeance until you've lovingly explored other areas—mound of Venus, pubic hair (see *Bush*), the outer and inner lips, the vagina, thighs, maybe some excursions to your breasts and nipples (here two hands are better than one: one above, one down there). From time to time, you can return to the clitoris with an up-and-down stroking of the shaft, a circling and gentle pulling of the clitoris itself. You can place the heel of your hand at the clitoris as you move one or several fingers in and out of the vagina. The amount of pressure, the speed of vibrating motions at the clitoris, and the intensity of vaginal penetration (if any) will generally mount as you come closer to coming.

Once you have come, try to avoid jumping up to attend to something else. Lie there and enjoy the waves; squeeze your thighs together; lazily stretch and roll your body around; *smile*.

Handmade orgasms are lovely, but you may want to investigate vibrators, dildos, whirlpool baths and shower heads (never shoot water up your vagina though), as well as indulging in some more fanciful inventions. We are told, for example, that the juicy side of an apple cut in half simulates some of the effects of oral sex. A number of women, with a kind of look-ma-no-hands bravado, report perfectly successful orgasms reached simply by alternately tightening and relaxing pelvic muscles (an excellent method, as we've indicated elsewhere, of lessening boredom on long plane or train trips).

Again, whatever pleases you is fine. This is particularly true of masturbation because, by definition, you are not concerned with pleasing (or offending) anyone but yourself. What you learn in masturbating, though, may very well help to make you a better lover when you are with a partner.

Menopause Menopause is the permanent cessation of menstruation, typically occurring between the ages of forty and sixty. As we discuss in *Growing older*, menopause for lesbians can be the entry into total sexual abandonment *sans* cramps, *sans* the taste of cotton, *sans* all the bloody interruptions female flesh is heir to. Many menopausal lesbians have learned that orgasm is the best of antidotes for any physical discomfort incurred during this time. Sometimes, however, physiological disturbances can cause psychological hang-ups during menopause. Lesbians do not generally (and certainly should never) associate loss of reproductive function with loss of sexual attractiveness.

Menstruation Even women intent upon procreation have for centuries nicknamed menstruation "the curse," as if some evil influence were operating. What causes menstruation is hardly supernatural: estrogenic hormones influence the thickening of uterine mucosa, the development of glandular secretions and increased blood supply, all in preparation for the uterus to receive and nurture a fertilized egg. When this does not occur— as is by far the majority of times among some 420 possibilities if a woman ovulates for 35 years—all this material is sloughed off in the form of menstrual blood, which flows (or trickles) down the vagina, necessitating the wearing of some collection device.

Men traditionally have had some trouble with "all that blood," which must account for the old religious proscriptions and the newer fad of scrambling for extragenital methods of getting it off. Lesbians, however, don't seem to have this trouble, probably because they, too, menstruate and accept it as being connected with their own bodies (though it can still be a nuisance or a bore, if not "the curse") and also because many women feel their sexiest near or at menses. Somebody up there may have had good intentions, since this is a time at which, at least theoretically, it is impossible to get pregnant—thus a time for unbridled, joyous sex. Alas, the plan (if it was one) never worked too well for straight women because so many straight men find menstruation scarey and "ucky."

There is no real reason to curb sex during menstruation. If the flow is heavy and hence a source of physical or psychological discomfort to either of you, wear a tampon. This will still allow for some amount of penetration if that's part of your scenario for the occasion, and, of course, it will create no impediment whatsoever to clitoral stimulation. You may well experience a lessening of flow during sexual activity anyway. In any event, the presence of a few towels should handle any problems.

Some lesbians take extra delight in lovemaking during menstruation. In addition to the possible heightened responsiveness we mentioned, there's the physical aspect of extra wetness and warmth, and the psychological excitement of sex—including going down and mutually enjoying it—at a time when women are commonly (but erroneously) considered "unclean."

Mirror-mirror "Mirror-mirror, on the wall, who's the fairest one of all?" For you, it will be your lover; for her, you (although we would hope that any well-adjusted woman will also like herself and hence her own body, too). It's fun, sexy and a great morale-booster for both of you to stand in front of a full-length mirror and admire each other. This can be done stark nude (with or without jewelry, feather boas or formidable-looking leather belts) purely as entertainment in and of itself, before or after sex. During sex mirrors can be especial fun, introducing you both to new-found pleasures as you watch what both of you are doing. If you're shy about having large mirrors permanently mounted in your bedroom, try keeping one in a closet and prop it up at a good vantage point when you want it. You could alternatively spread some pillows and blankets in front of a large mirror that is already mounted in some other room.

Many lesbians find "mirror-mirror" a delightful love game to play when fully clothed. It's probably the best way to check out how you really look together and—particularly in happy moments when you are just about to go out for an evening—it's reassuring for you to appreciate the in-love image everyone else will see.

Mound of Venus The mound of Venus (*mons veneris, mons pubis*) is that marvelously sensitive little heap of flesh that covers the pubic bone and leads directly to the vulvar area. It responds to stroking, kneading, kissing, mound-to-mound rubbing, feather-light caresses, tonguing and nibbling, the lapping of warm water (see *Water, water, everywhere*), and just about any variation lovers can invent.

When time, occasion, the presence of clothes, or other situations prohibit "total" sex, the mound of Venus is an excellent focal point while dancing, hugging, or playing private games with one hand on the table and the other exploring those parts of your lover discreetly hidden by the tablecloth.

Multiple orgasms Women's capacity to make love for seemingly endless stretches of time, coming and then coming again (and again), has always been a source of wonderment and envy to men. It's undoubtedly a principal reason behind centuries of oppression: woman's place is in the kitchen; if she is freed to enjoy the bedroom, men will be worn out.

While lesbians certainly have their share of problems, the ability to come more than once—or enjoying several peak waves of orgasm rather than one—is certainly not among them. Secure in the arms of another woman, someone like her, the lesbian is both free at last and free *to* last.

Of course, being able to come more than once doesn't mean you have to, or that there's something wrong if you don't. Many female lovers, engrossed in their own rhythm and pace of lovemaking, prolong orgasm because the whole process of sexual communication is so enjoyable. Then, when they do come, it's so fantastic that drifting off to sleep in each other's arms seems more right than anything else. It's as much a matter of mood and temperament as physiology, so answer to what you both *want* to do rather than what you both *can* do.

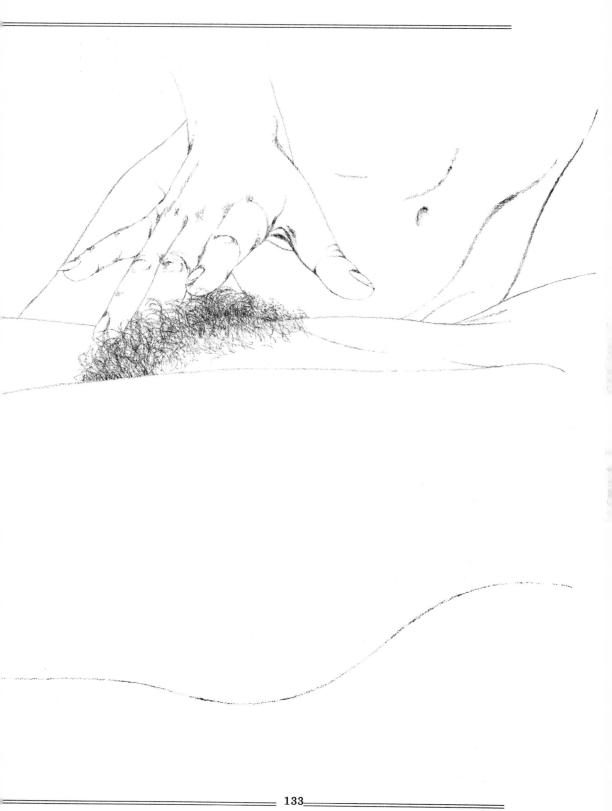

Myths *All* of the misconceptions about lesbianism—about lesbian life-styles as well as sexuality—come about through unthinking acceptance of the masculine as the touchstone of normal behavior, as the center of the universal reality. Suggestions to the contrary are tantamount to heresy, reminiscent of the popular response to Galileo's demonstration that it is the earth that revolves around the sun, and not the other way round. It is still largely *unthinkable* that a woman can operate without a man; *unthinkable* that her natural inclinations might radiate from feminine rather than masculine instincts; *unthinkable* that whole days might go by when a thought of men and their ways never crosses her mind:

A woman tells a (liberated) male friend that she's a lesbian. He turns pale; he tries to be cool, but can't restrain himself from saying, "Oh, but what a *waste!*"

A lesbian couple are trying to have an intelligent discussion about lesbianism with a straight friend. The friend finally admits that the truly burning question still bothering her is which of the pair plays the woman and which the man.

A lesbian is giving a talk on the benefits of women loving women; benefits, she points out, that include supportive friendships as well as erotic relationships. For the hour she speaks she never once mentions any emotions but love, loving kindness and the feelings of sisterhood. She never once refers to the opposite sex. When she concludes her presentation and opens the floor for discussion, a woman in the back of the room stands up and shouts angrily, "Why do you lesbians *hate men* so much?"

A lesbian who is a college professor comes out in her profession. A male colleague is quite obviously turned on by her revelation. He begins to find excuses to drop in on her at her office almost daily, and through much conversational contrivance to include the subject of lesbianism in the discussion. The lesbian charitably assumes that he is distressed by his ignorance and hungry for enlightenment. But at last even her long-enduring patience snaps. "You know," he says on his last visit to her office, "it's really strange how everytime I take my wife to a party there's always some lesbian there who makes a pass at her." The lesbian professor, with a great show of sympathy, replies: "Really? Oh dear, I'm sorry. As you probably know—since it is such a well-known fact—lesbians very seldom make advances to straight women. . . ."

A lesbian pediatrician has, since the child's infancy, treated the daughter of a friend. When the girl enters puberty the mother abruptly switches her to the care of a male physician. With the delicacy of a bull in a china shop, the mother explains to her (former) friend that she believed it a kindly act to "remove the temptation" of an increasingly lovely young girl from the doctor's way.

A lesbian who has successfully worked with delinquent girls for twelve years, and has, on several occasions, been publicly commended for her work by the organization's officials, is moved by the dictates of conscience to come out in the context of the Gay Rights movement. Within twenty-four hours she is fired from her job and told that she "will never work again" in the youth-rehabilitation professions: a lesbian is an "inappropriate role-model" for impressionable youngsters.

A composite myth is that because lesbians are not "men's women" they are not women at all and therefore must "be" men, or be like men; since lesbians are sexually unavailable to men, they are without sexual function, they are "wasted"; that lesbian relationships are a mirror image of male–female relationships; that because lesbians love women they must necessarily hate men; that lesbians are indiscriminately sexually aggressive and promiscuous—as, in the macho imagination, men presumably are; that lesbians can be sexually aroused by children to such an extent that they abandon all ethical, moral and professional standards to lust—as, sadly, the statistics on child abuse show, men do; that lesbians are into conversion of the young and, if not, their mere presence among the "unconverted" can act like a virus: like a bad cold, it is presumed, lesbianism can be "caught." These die-hard attitudes could be labeled simply ludicrous and dismissed as such were it not for the appalling damage they have caused and the lives they have ruined. Some parents of lesbians would generally still prefer to lose their daughters entirely than have the neighbors know that their daughter-the-doctor is also a lesbian daughter-the-doctor. Courts of law would in many instances rather a child have no mother at all than have a lesbian mother. Professions would rather reject gifted women workers than use the resources of a gifted lesbian worker. Besides fear, however, we wonder if there is not also an element of "thrill" popularly associated with lesbianism—that the lesbian is a creature so fabulous, so exotic she has magical (thus, disruptive) qualities and, like the famous unicorn, must be captured and contained. Is it possible that what people fear most about lesbians is lesbians' understanding of *pleasure*?

Navel "Belly button" is more than baby-talk for navel. For many women the button seems to signal through direct wiring to the vulva, as well as all around the body.

You might try deepening the natural depression by cupping both your hands around your lover's navel as you slip the tip of your tongue in, out and around. Big toes, thumbs, fingers, as well as toys such as a feather or the tip of a dildo or dildo-shaped vibrator, are also useful signal-makers.

Navel fingering and tonguing can also serve as a good substitute for breast-play on occasions when (for example, prior to menstruation) your lover's breasts may be too tender.

Nose As we've suggested in other places in this book, there isn't a single portion of your body for which you cannot find a sexual use and that cannot, properly stimulated, be sexually aroused. While your tongue is busy licking her labia, vagina or clitoris or your entire mouth is sucking on her vulva, you can use your nose as far as you can to reach into her bush, pressing particularly hard at the base of the clitoris. Such pressure cannot be constant, of course, since you have to breathe, so keep your nose out of action until you feel her beginning to reach orgasm. In this instant, the radius of her pleasure will be widened by the sudden pressure of your nose—wonderfully effective if the "nose job" is a surprise to your lover. The area for the nose job can be extended if you're able to stretch her lower abdomen's skin up with the flat of your hand. This technique also pulls all the vulva up and out, stretching sensitivity as well as the anatomy.

Nudity As we've said before, women have usually been considered, by most of human-kind, most places and at most times, the more esthetically pleasing of the two genders. It can surely come as no surprise that two naked women making love can sometimes approach the height of ecstasy just looking at each other. Combine that with touching, kissing and making it sexually and any uninitiated reader may grasp at least some understanding of why lesbians feel that their sex life is the best.

While we're one hundred percent for nudity—not just for sex, but also for sunbathing, swimming, or wandering about the house when you like—we don't advocate it as a total life-style or as a too-hastily-achieved prerequisite to falling into bed together. Clothing excites the imagination about what it's draping (even when you've seen it and know), and there is something both romantic and arousing about seeing your lover partially clothed as the two of you slowly undress.

You might enjoy some occasional parading-around in, say, bikini-style bra and panties. More theatrical types may prefer garter belts and boots (or stockings), but a lot of lesbians find this off-putting because they are reminded of male brothel imagery.

As always, what both of *you* like is O.K., even going to bed in T-shirts rather than the altogether if that's what turns the two of you on.

Orgasm There is no such thing as a frigid lesbian. Unless they are temporarily incapacitated—stoned, ill, quite preoccupied or the like—lesbians *always* reach orgasm in their lovemaking, and frequently experience the joy of reaching it again and again in the same session. Orgasm has as many definitions as there are lesbians, but its effect is an interplay of physiology

and poetry in which what "actually" happens in the body's nervous, vascular, glandular and muscular systems is psychologically transformed into something almost magical, mystical, goddess-like. The event's essential nature is a reflection of that same human quality that transforms "having sex" into "making love." And if that quality is—as we, along with the rest of the world, tend to believe—most highly developed in women, then the joy of sex as experienced by two women together must epitomize both the physiologic and poetic meanings of orgasm.

Out in the open   If so many people enjoy napping out in the open air, then why do so few of them make love under the spreading chestnut tree?

Perhaps because it's growing fifteen meters from an interstate highway. That's a good enough reason, but even the most dedicated urbanite knows of some secret woodland place, often surprisingly close to the city. Apart from insuring privacy the only other precaution needed is a quilt or blanket, unless twigs and ants turn you on.

The clock is on your side, for once, so you can peel off each other's clothes with the kind of deliberation you might sense if time had stopped and evening will never come. You've swapped a ceiling for the sky, so take turns cradling each other so that both of you can stare at it, revel in it, invent stories about creatures and events the clouds form as they float serenely above you, should they start to come to mind.

What you do—hands, mouths, thighs, toys—is less important than how you do it. Pause to drink, smoke or eat. Touch the grass as well as each other. Sprawl carelessly as you breathe in the scent of clean, country air. Share some secret thoughts about how it might be to live on that blanket forever.

You don't have to be in a forest: your secret place might be a deserted beach (watch out for the sand), a lawn (given an adequate fence) or a boat anchored some distance from the shore (be sure you're securely anchored, or the drifting away may be of another variety). What matters is freeing your imagination, building and sharing new fantasies.

Of course, if you live in the country, where open sky and clean air are old hat to you, your secret place might be a large hotel in the biggest city you can get to. A place where you can marvel at the smog and noise, and make love in a bathtub that's only one-half the size of yours at home.

Perfumes   Some women prefer the Parisian variety; others, natural essences such as musk oil; and plenty of women would rather smell like soap and water.

Our straight counterpart, *The Joy of Sex*, goes into some fairly rapturous details about *cassolette*, the "natural perfume" that comes from the whole body: hair, skin, breasts, armpits, genitals. However, in several references it's made fairly clear that this is more of a male turn-on ("some men respond violently to it"; it is a "secret weapon to an extent that women in America don't seem to realize—French women know better").

We find this an interesting interpretation, since France was and remains the keystone of the perfume industry (that is, the pretty-smelling commercial stuff) and *The Joy of Sex* admits that women have "the keener sense of smell" and "on the whole tend to notice if a man smells right [*sic*] or wrong [*sic*]."

As we've said elsewhere (for example, see *Armpits*) lesbians do respond to odors characteristic of their partner, and the changing scents of vulvas in action further fan the fire; interestingly, what you smell may have a smokey quality to it. Too, many women report being turned on by the smell of slightly sweaty feet or a navel with a touch of "fuzz." Their lover's scent lingering on pyjamas or lingerie can be a powerful stimulant to many lesbians.

On the whole, however, we believe that lesbians—like all women—are less "natural smell-conscious" than men. Or, put another, more appropriate and accurate way, women are fussier about what they consider agreeable odors. Hence it is entirely possible that women in general buy and use perfume and colognes not to cover up the animal but to enhance the human. We know of many lesbian lovers who have admitted to taking lunch-hour breaks in the perfume areas of department stores, happily sniffing their absent lover's favorite scent—her olfactory trademark, as it were.

Pillow talk Pillow talk can mean anything from muttering "sweet nothings" about your lover's hair, eyes, kisses, to giving full vent to your most salacious fantasies about what you're going to do to her or what you want her to do to you. The words can look improbably coarse (or even too aggressive?) on the printed page, but sound altogether different in the warmth of a bed where passionate lovemaking is going on. "Fuck me harder" (or, conversely, "Slow down a little") counts for pillow talk as each of you forms raw sensation into words.

Lovers need to communicate, and the more communication the better. As we've stated elsewhere in this book, real liberation means being able to say what you want rather than being bound by wiggling and thrashing in the hope your partner is a good mind reader. The kinds of things you say will vary: some lesbians are turned on by the raunchiest kind of "dirty words"; others prefer a more romanticized version. Finding what works best for the two of you is part of

developing a fulfilling relationship—understanding what makes each other tick. You may both conclude, for example, that pillow talk is *not* your cup of tea; that verbal communication is better saved for other situations, or that transforming moans into words seems too hokey an intellectualization. That, too, is all right, although we'd suggest not putting it down before you've tried it.

It is really essential that, just as with the rest of your lovemaking, pillow talk remain a treasured part of the private world you and your partner create in bed. What's said is not meant for public consumption, nor should you ever use (misuse) the material to taunt, tease or provoke your lover. Pillow talk tends to flow best when you are at your most exposed, most vulnerable moments.

Play Sex play and playfulness in sex are central themes of this book. What we mean by "play" here is plain *play*: recreation, leisure activities, the pursuit of pure fun, sharing an escape from everyday cares.

Lesbians often work harder than other women. They tend to be unusually ambitious in pursuit of their careers or professions. This is not hard to understand. They are in active rebellion against a male-dominated society, and work hard to actualize their belief that they are just as capable and just as deserving as the male colleagues they must almost inevitably compete against. Also, freed from the expectation that their fulfillment will derive from some man's (husband's) success, lesbians tend to engage themselves in their work with energetic passion, liking it and expecting (and often obtaining) gratification from it. They neither expect nor want to be supported by someone else, so they work to obtain the material comforts many straight women still expect from the men they marry.

Like everyone else, lesbians have to run their homes, sometimes even raising children. So far that all makes for a busy life, but on top there is the fact that, except in the most enlightened communities, and even there one can't always be sure, lesbians are often discriminated against. Most often discrimination is subtle (though nonetheless hurtful), such as slightly snide comments in the supermarket; occasionally it is major, such as losing a job (or chance for advancement) because you are known to be, or even just suspected of being, gay.

Taken together, these problems of a lesbian life-style will, in one sense, be doubled when two women in love decide to enter a relationship. In another sense, the problems are lessened by the act and the effects of sharing: being a lesbian herself, your lover will also probably be ambitious in her pursuit of a satisfying work life, she will expect to support herself and she too will keep house.

Because time is precious and pressures considerable it does help to set aside generous portions of time for sheer *play*. Even when you are engaged in some project that absolutely demands working when you shouldn't be, be sure to set aside some time for play—even if it's just a stroll around the block and one drink at a friendly bar before you relax over dinner together. It sometimes helps to structure this in advance, and it helps to remind both of you that neither has forgotten the other. For example, you may have to shut yourself away for several hours of concentrated work, but at a fixed time you'll be getting together for tea or cocktails. Or you may decide to play all day Saturday and then work all day Sunday. Agreement is important—that is, mutual understanding of what the work is and why it must be done during what should be playtime; how you can mesh your schedules to accommodate each other and how you'd like to play.

There is, of course, no rule that you must always play together. Time alone for playing—even if it's just lounging about and day-dreaming—is also a necessary restorative. And it can put you both in a better mood for sharing the playtime you have together.

Pornography Almost all pornography is written by men for men. Hardly any pornography reflects the realities of female sexuality, especially lesbian sexuality: understandably, since it is a two-dimensional synthesis of male fantasy which a realistic version of the female point of view is not intended to interrupt. Its subject matter is the celebration of the cock and the sexual exploitation of women. Much pornography is about male fantasies of violence involving women, but a different scene that is almost *de rigueur* in porn film and literature is explicit sex between lesbians. Typically, such a scene is resolved by the introduction of a massive erection between the two women; and, once again, it is demonstrated that all they ever needed was a good fuck by a good dick. Even in "serious" literature the lesbian is used pornographically to demonstrate male sexual superiority: D. H. Lawrence's *The Fox* is a blatant example.

Definitions of what is pornographic change according to time, culture and the individual, but lesbians always seem to come off badly. In the most celebrated pornography/lesbian prosecution of this century, that of Radclyffe Hall's rather stuffy, rather sentimental novel *The Well of Loneliness* in 1928, the basis for finding the charge of obscenity proven was explained by the magistrate, Sir Charles Biron, thus: "The mere fact that a book deals with unnatural offences between women does not make it obscene. It might even have a strong moral influence. But in the present case there is not one word which suggests that anyone with the horrible tendencies described is in the least degree blameworthy. All the characters are presented as attractive people and put forward with admiration."

Even now, to show lesbians as real people with real lives is distasteful to many people. Biron's view still obtains. In the past few years writers of fiction have adopted the raw porn formula of including at least one lesbian episode within the course of the novel and their portrayal of lesbianism is not substantially different from the pornographer's: a straight woman experiments with lesbianism with a "real" lesbian and the experience is scored off as a "temporary aberration" or, at best, as an adventure-holiday from heterosexuality. Or, again, the lesbian is shown as a monstrosity of sexuality who lures the lady into her net with her awesome seductive powers. Again, this fiction is based on fantasies of lesbianism rather than on any recognizable reality (see *Clit lit* for a description of what we mean by a true lesbian literature). Lesbian pornography—written by and for lesbians and meant to stimulate lesbian sexual fantasies—does not, as far as we know, exist. We wonder, in fact, if pornography is something the lesbian imagination necessarily needs. But, to be honest, it is true that many lesbians do use both soft and hard porn intended for men to turn on with. Some lesbians masturbate with their eyes on the *Playboy* centerfold, some get excited by explicit heterosexual fucking passages in porn fiction. The reasons for this are complex (see *Fantasy*), but it doesn't seem to matter where and how the sexual stimulation of the woman in pornographic scenes is brought about as long as female feeling and perspective are included. As far as we know, however, there are very few if any lesbians who are turned on, as many men are, by scenes of violence.

Our point is that if you like it, if it stimulates you, if it's useful in geting your juices flowing, then porn is simply another aphrodisiac and should be treated as such. If you feel any guilt about enjoying looking at pictures of beautiful girls with astonishing breasts or reading about orgasms that shake the chandeliers from the ceiling, if it especially worries you that your pleasure is coming from residues of sexism in your character—that you might be taking on "male-identification"—then stop it. Keep in mind Mark Twain's remark about censorship: that a girl was never ruined by a book.

Promiscuity Although some lesbians are sexually active with varying partners, the word "promiscuity" as it could describe the sex lives of many males simply isn't applicable. Lesbians on the whole seem to be more intent on forming relationships than on having sex for sex's sake.

Puberty In most cultures puberty is marked by special rites. For girls in America and other countries that take their cues from American movies and TV, these rites (at least heretofore) consisted largely of hanging up your baseball mitt, shelving your chemistry set and learning how to become the literal or figurative cheerleader for boys engaged in physical and mental activities of a competitive nature.

Junior and senior high school is hardly the barrel of laughs senior citizens prefer to remember, but for young lesbians the suffering assumes awesome and terribly poignant proportions. Still half-trapped in the childlike resolution of wanting to be a boy so it would be O.K. to love women (and baseball and chemistry), you watch helplessly as your flat chest grows less flat. You're left with the sinking feeling that there's no way to get out of this situation. Your sense of being different begins to play terrible tricks on your mind, and every between-class snicker becomes a sign that They, too, know. And the more you try to compensate by editing the yearbook, taking scholastic honors, swimming faster than half the boys, winning the lead part in a play or wearing more lipstick than anyone else the wider the gulf seems to be.

The shower room after gym class is a special torture chamber. All adolescent girls have trouble adjusting to their new bodies, but the feeling of gawky strangeness is compounded in the young lesbian who feels exposed not only in her own nakedness but by the blush-making eroticism she may experience surrounded by nude females.

It's a time when you feel a difference in crushes, too. They rapidly become less vague, less a matter of undefined longing. The time for reckoning is just about at hand, yet teenagers struggling for their identity are most often as afraid of being "different" sexually as they are in any other way.

Amazingly, people seem to survive the turmoil of puberty. But the adult who can't remember how ardent—let alone loving, responsible, grown-up and downright sexy—she or he felt about so-and-so at age 16 suffers from an extremely faulty memory. Lesbians tend to remember. And it helps to make them more accepting of all people struggling for identity.

Quickies Any sexual encounter, with yourself or with another, that is short and sweet qualifies as a quickie. A quickie can have the same intensity and blissful realizations as the most prolonged sexual orchestration; sometimes it can be better if it suits the excitement of the moment. A quickie is based on lust that can't and won't wait. In some respects it resembles what goes on during dressed sex, although, as in dressed sex, wearing clothes is not the object. The clothes are simply there, and there may be neither time nor opportunity to shed them.

You're working in your office and a hot late-afternoon lust assails you: you speed to the ladies' room, lock yourself in a cubicle, unzip, get off with your ever-loyal hand. You meet someone at a party and desire is instantly communicated between you. If the opportunity ever comes again with her it will be qualitatively different from this time: you exchange names (addresses and phone numbers can wait) and if your hostess's bedroom doesn't have a lock, you make a rush for the bathroom and get inside each other's pants with your hands. With a little more time (and if you can make yourself deaf to the impatient pounding at the door), taking turns you can go down on each other. A quickie can be especially satisfying in warm weather out of doors: up against a tree, in sweet-smelling grass or, literally, in the bushes. Long-time lovers, entirely knowledgeable about what to do where and how and with what, often make quickies a matter of course in their relationship. Setting the alarm clock ten or fifteen minutes ahead can organize quickies in your lives and start the day with something a lot more energizing than instant coffee.

Roles Very easily "roles" becomes a catchall to constrict people by defining them within just one of their normal behavior patterns (who's the butch, who's the femme?) or just as easily gets them entangled in a series of other people's restrictions: one shouldn't always be dominant, one shouldn't always be submissive, getting stuck in the same old rut is wrong.

Maybe the confusion is with role-*playing*, which frequently amounts to presenting your self quite differently from how you yourself perceive that self, or half-consciously widening the gap between your espoused theories and your theories in action. For example, behold Maryann, who detests gossiping but then proceeds to dish every lesbian east of the Hudson River; or Beverly, who just adores gay men but, when out of earshot, customarily refers to them as "faggot pricks."

Roles can just as easily define a set of responsibilities, which, for a lesbian couple, frequently reflects a suitable division of labor. By "suitable," we mean whatever you both decide is appropriate. If she majored in math and you can't add two and two, who's the more logical choice for handling joint banking matters? If you type and she pecks with one finger, who's the more logical choice for preparing anything you need to have typewritten?

What makes for satisfaction in any intimate relationship between lesbians is that both partners consider the trade-off equal. For example, cooking every night is not in anyone's terms equal to carrying out the garbage; balancing a checkbook once a month is not equivalent to typing one short letter once a year.

You have to start from a shared definition of what responsibility is. For most straight couples it is an ingrained part of the total picture: the husband works and balances checkbooks, repairs faulty

wiring, or hires someone to do it, arranges all business and financial matters, pays bills, buys things—or provides the money for doing so; the wife keeps house and bears and raises children, cooks and does the dishes, reports what needs to be fixed or bought. The roles are set, although of course that's exactly what many straight women are rebelling against.

Lesbians, more than any other group of women, have the opportunity not just of throwing off the whole worn concept of roles *per se* but also of freely structuring their own sets of responsibilities within an intimate relationship.

While trading off can work well as long as the trade-offs are mutually considered to be equivalent, there are other tasks that can be *shared*. Even if one of you is the superior cook, the other can surely manage enough dinners so that neither of you feels trapped in a role; even if one of you has the more convenient working schedule, the other can surely manage sometimes to go to the supermarket; even if you don't know how to rewire a busted socket, you can stand by with screwdriver and wirecutter.

Finally, having no stake in the "me Tarzan, you Jane" game—except in fun—loving lesbians can role reverse easily. If she is, either by natural bent or by profession, the nurse of the household, take special pains to quell your fear of blood and be prepared to take over the next medical emergency. It will help her to understand how loved she is, and you to understand what love is about: sharing.

Romance   Romance is sex with love. Sex without love is not romance. *Inter alia*, this book is about romance.

Sadomasochism   Although S and M enjoys a considerable vogue in gay male circles, its relative rarity among lesbians seems well attested. Witness the following classified advertisement which ran in *The Advocate* (a widely circulated gay magazine published on the West Coast):

> Are there any lesbians into experimenting with S & M
> or Bondage and Discipline? Or have you been interested
> but too shy to do anything? We'd appreciate hearing
> from you for a future ADVOCATE article.

It's our distinct impression that not many lesbians are into sadomasochism—probably because women are fighting hard to escape centuries of what feels like slavery, as well as male-imposed myths of martyrdom and women's liking to be beaten up. Most women recoil at equating eroticism with playing rough in scenes that bear a resemblance to Nazi experimental stations.

Of course, fantasy is another matter—strutting around in boots or masturbating while imagining you're being ravished by a wild beast (female, of course), or kissing your lover and thinking how nice it might be utterly to devour her—but that is pretty tame stuff (ask anyone, gay or straight, who is into the S and M scene) and would not pass for real sadomasochism.

However, what is rare still does exist and there is no sound reason for denying yourself the S and M experience if it interests you—and if your partner willingly consents. But you do need to be careful.

Seduction For a word that literally means "to lead aside," seduction has certainly fallen upon a bad reputation. The small child who smiles winningly at the local grocer, who then gladly parts with a candy malt ball, is engaging in seduction. The psychotherapist who accepts a gift from a client is being seduced and so is a client who sticks with an incompatible psychotherapist because of the latter's dire predictions of the outcome should the sessions be terminated. High-school kids butter up their parents to borrow the family car; door-to-door salesmen seduce

status-conscious housewives into believing their family's lives will be ruined if a certain encyclopedia is not prominently displayed in the special bookcase that comes with it. Whole nations have sometimes been seduced into thinking God has appointed them to save the world from the clutches of some other nation.

Among lesbians intent upon getting someone into bed, seduction is very rarely a one-way affair: there is no seductress and no seductee, but rather a mutual interplay of courting behavior that evolves and re-forms into activities that prove the most effective turn-ons.

In the game of exploration and discovery, one may use anything from the poetry of Sappho to statistics about women Olympic medal-winners. Some women turn rapturous over discussions of epicurean tables, others respond to subtle compliments about their own voluptuousness. Plays, politics and philosophy all count for fair game; you feel yourself melt when she says: "Yes, I see what you mean."

Conversation, however, is supplemented by other things: your own presentation-of-the-rose scene, dinner by candlelight, a trip to the country, the sharing of a concert, hockey game, ceremony, or political lecture that is meaningful to both of you. Plus—perhaps above all—the exchange of less-tangible signals: spontaneous sighs (don't try to fake one), a long, searching look in which eyes do not avert, shared laughter for the sheer joy of it.

Which one of you will touch first? Don't worry about it; don't "plot" too thoroughly; it will happen. Possibly in one of those laughing spells, as you each seize the other's arm for support and then discover you are still holding on. There is no ritual for seduction, it seems to revolve around presenting yourself as you are (although, obviously, you play down the less desirable aspects of your personality) and making links with her as she presents herself.

You don't have to be new to each other, though, to recreate the thrill of seduction. Lesbians can and do create their own rituals for seduction once they're together as partners. Bringing out the feather boa, dancing nude for each other, bathing each other and playing-out made-up theater scenes can all take on special meanings for lovers and are among the activities that bring more joy to sex.

Sexism Sexism is a totally unfounded belief in the superiority of males. A sexist-*manquée* is a woman who believes in sexism. Some people date the advent of history from the institutionalization of sexism. Some people date the beginning of civilization from the institutionalization of the sexist-*manquée*. Heterosexism, the totally inflexible belief in the superiority, both natural and esthetic, of heterosexual sex and life-style, is a by-product of sexism. A heterosexist, male or female, is somebody who just hasn't had much experience of sexuality.

Sitting pretty Both of you naked, you sitting in an armless chair, she astride your thighs, open. Your breasts and nipples touching, your fingers inside her vagina, inside her anus, on her clitoris. A good time to use a vibrator. Another variation happens on the bed or on the floor: both of you sitting upright, your legs entwined so that your vulvas are wide open and "kissing" each other.

Sixty-nining   Going down on each other simultaneously—one aspect of *Sucking*.

Skin   There may be some microscopic portion of the female epidermis that is incapable of responding to erotic stimulation, but we doubt it. One of the most delightful aspects of knowing the skin's capacity for arousal is the finesse you can acquire in enjoying sexual play with your lover nearly any place, nearly any time.

 Generally, it is the lightest touch that excites the most response and some of the most responsive parts of the skin are the most public: the hands, fingers, neck, crook of the elbow, inner wrist. Practiced lovers can describe their partner's erotic geography in detail, and can imagine their fingertips on voyages of discovery. Almost imperceptibly to those around you (in a theater, on a bus, in a restaurant) your index finger can begin to circle the whorls of her fingerprint, gradually widening the circle, extending the touch to include the entire underside of her finger. This touch alone, on a single finger, can bring some women to a high pitch of arousal.

Lightly brushing your fingers up and down her inner arm, as if you were painting a design there, further awakens the skin's sensitivity. Some lovers declare that they have developed an erotic code of tactile stimulation, a veritable language of sensual love.

The least exposed areas of the skin are the most ardent in response; the palm, the underside of the arm, the arch of the foot, the inner thigh. In privacy, fingers can give way to the tip of the tongue; the light caress and tickle can give way to deep fondling, squeezing (especially of inner thighs and breasts). The lips, too, are sensitive to more than a kiss: stroking her lips with a finger can create a unique tension, sometimes resulting in her mouth's capture of your finger for vigorous sucking. To be effective, tactile stimulation must be persistent and locate on one area of the skin at a time. It must also, initially, be very light, very gentle, very tender, only gradually building to deeper manipulation. There exists, too, a sometimes comic ritual known as the "lesbian handshake." You begin with the conventional handshake grip but making sure that there is space between the palms of your hands. Then you quickly release your middle finger and tickle her palm, stroke or probe it.

Standing up Standing-up sex calls for some ingenuity and can enliven the shared experience of even the most uninhibited lovers. Handwork, dildo- and vibrator-sharing, thigh-rubbing are all suitable techniques and part of the fun is maintaining enough control so that you don't go into a "little death" swoon and collapse; leaning against a wall may be necessary. If one is agile enough to arch backwards sufficiently the other can make effective mouth-to-clitoris contact.

Sucking Because lesbians love women, lust for women, *like* women more than anybody else they have fewer hang-ups about oral sex than anybody else. Lovemaking with your mouth on that "other" mouth can be the quintessence of the lesbian sexual experience: with your lips and tongue you declare your love; with the same lips and tongue you demonstrate it, speaking, in the most exquisite of non-verbal languages, of how she is desirable *there. In that way.* It is no surprise to lesbians that oral sex is widely considered to be the most intimate way of making love.

Your mouth on her cunt, hers on yours; or, together, you practice sixty-nine. Sixty-nine, however, is most successfully achieved when you and your lover have become deeply familiar with each other's patterns of response and even then there is usually some difficulty. When you yourself are racing toward climax, your body stiffening or wildly rocking and you're longing to abandon yourself to yelling, moaning or gnashing your teeth it is almost impossible to keep your tongue concentrated in her cunt. Sixty-nine, therefore, is usually best kept for some fun foreplay, or used as a langorous finishing-off when both of you are already thoroughly satisfied.

Too many lesbians, however, have been brainwashed into believing that only in sixty-nine can perfect sexual mutuality be achieved; and that taking turns is somehow politically disgraceful in its expression of "active" and "passive" roles. The sexual reality tells a different story. While you are down on your partner, your tongue speeding from tantalizing licks to a literal wallowing in her cunt, she, in response, is increasing her own activity. She is definitely not lying there like a knocked-out baby doll while you get your jollies off; she moves, she talks dirty, she caresses your head; she can even offer a part of herself for you to squeeze between your legs—a hand, a thigh, an arm. More than likely lesbians' mistaken notions of what is "active" and what is "passive" are a cartoon of heterosexual coupling, in which the wife lies still and endures ("For God and Country") while her husband gets off.

Going down can be accomplished from several positions: the old missionary (you slither down her body until your face is between her spread legs); from the side (she lies flat, her legs spread; you

approach from the side with the top of your head pointing toward her feet); from the bottom up (you slide up between her legs). She can also lie with her legs overhanging the side or bottom of the bed while you crouch on your knees. Another method, highly favored by women who like to watch each other while they make love, involves her straddling your breasts (the weight is on her knees) and bringing

her cunt to your mouth. In this position, the one who is getting it has control of almost all pressure and contact points and releases all four hands: so much for the "passive" recipient of sex!

The "active" lover shouldn't attack all at once. You should approach her cunt stealthily; let it wait, anticipate. Tongue, gently nibble, kiss the nearby areas—thighs, belly, navel, bush. You hint at things to come. You part her pubic hair with your fingers and implant quick kisses with your lips over the entire vulva; then the vulva's lips, still keeping your tongue out of it for the moment. When your tongue comes into play at first you present just the tip, sliding it back and forth just inside the vulva's lips. Very gradually you give her more, glancing first at the vaginal opening, slipping next up to the clitoris which, at this stage, you only circle delicately, making promises, before you return to the vaginal opening, moving your tongue quickly in and out.

Until now, the tongue has been used in a pointed position, not too far out. Now, you let it hang loose, as far out as is comfortable. Using your tongue's whole flat breadth, sweep from the vagina up to the clitoris which you encircle with your lips and begin, lightly at first, to suck. As you suck, you rotate your mouth, around and around the clitoris, increasing pressure on the surrounding inner labia as you move. You stop; again, quickly, you extend your tongue and dart it back and forth, snake-like, within the labia and back to the in-and-out action in the vagina.

Most women like to be finished off with concentrated, hard, sucking and tongue washes over and around the clitoris. But overly direct stimulation of the clitoris can be painful and impede (or even prevent) orgasm. The degree of pressure, the amount of action and—crucially—*where* the pressure and action take place is something you learn to sense as your partner signals by moving, grasping, pulling or squeezing with her thighs. Or—this is real liberation—by telling you.

Lesbians can learn to move freely from one form of oral–genital sex to another. Very freely; with abandonment even, as self-confidence, openness and intimacy increase. Or, freedom may mean sometimes just staying with what you've learned is mutually pleasing and waiting comfortably until you both sense it's time for variations. For instance, some lesbians some of the time may want penetration and the feeling of a full vagina just as they're about to come from oral–genital stimulation. This is easy to give your partner with fingers or dildo. In the straddle position (with the one who's getting it kneeling over her lover's breasts) it is especially easy for the woman on the bottom to insert a finger or a dildo as she tongues and sucks. This may pose some of the timing hazards of sixty-nine, but it's worth investigation by lesbians intent on doubling their pleasure.

Therapy Since homosexuality is not considered a mental disorder (even the American Psychiatric Association says so), why would lesbians go into psychotherapy? For the same kinds of reasons anybody else might: interpersonal conflicts, situational crises, the feeling that you're "unfocused" or not "goal-directed," experiences of loss or grief, phobias and anxieties, a sense of diffuse depression, vocational problems, and other more or less specific complaints—or, just about as frequently, a desire for better understanding of the self. A kind of universal goal, shared by most clients and most psychotherapists alike (regardless of theoretical background), is that of improved self-actualization and self-esteem as precursors to, or concomitants of, more satisfying interpersonal relationships.

In short, one does not have to be "neurotic" to be in therapy (although some people may be—*if* one accepts classic descriptions of, say, obsessive-compulsive patterning—and hence some lesbians, being people, might be so categorized by themselves or others); nor does one have to be on the brink of what traditionalists may call a "psychotic break" to be in therapy (although some people, including lesbians) may define their anguish in just those terms.

What then, given that lesbians are essentially people, makes therapy such a different proposition?

First of all, gay women are *women*. As discussed in many other sections of this book, women have for countless centuries been subjected to both outright and subtle oppression that can make them prime candidates for feeling they are second-rate (or, conversely, simply too precious or pristine to act on the human urges that beset them). Gay women are also subjected to the explicit and implicit societal messages that—while being a woman is bad enough —being *gay* is even worse. Thus problems for which lesbians seek therapy are very often not intrapsychic at all, but rather a reaction or series of reactions to externals. Yes, Virginia, it *is* out there and not in your head!

But the pain is not "out there." It is felt inside you, and experienced in levels that can range from mild discomfort to intense anguish. Although we make no claim that therapy is the only—or even necessarily in all cases the best—method for dealing with this pain, we do believe it is a viable course and one that at least may merit a trial.

Where to look? A tough problem for anyone shopping for a suitable therapist, but tougher still for the lesbian: a woman who has a *right* to undergo therapy with someone sympathetic to her life-style. Gay, lesbian and feminist referral services (now located in most major cities) can be of help. But even that is no absolute guarantee. Quick perusal of newspapers published by women or gays or even "straight" presses in larger cities like New York will reveal a host of "feminist therapists." Consider: where did they come from? that is, are they qualified professional therapists genuinely committed to feminism and sympathetic to the aspirations of gay females, or are they self-styled personal counselors who wouldn't know a civil right from a dead goldfish but who know very well when to jump on a bandwagon that promises new-found riches? Keep in mind that you have a right to ask about your prospective therapist's attitudes, as well as her (or his) credentials.

Which brings us to a ticklish subject: credentials. Many people argue that anybody (that is, anybody with "the talent") can be a therapist; that is, that a little exposure to being in a group, being in individual therapy, and perhaps even taking a short crash-course in psychologizing can turn a person into a qualified therapist. We understand this attitude as it reflects a reaction to some of the bumbling Frankensteinism of inept and unenlightened professionals, and we appreciate the worth of many aspects of peer counseling and the very real value of some leaderless groups (see, for example, *Consciousness raising*). We are not even across-the-board opposed to training lay people to act in some psychotherapeutic capacities (when they are *really* trained, and *really* supervised by qualified personnel). We do, however, maintain that there is an essential difference in focus and depth between therapies of these sorts and psychotherapy in which the credentialed therapist possesses not only the "right" attitudes and the most sympathetic approach but also the years of special training and supervised clinical practice that enable her (or him) to assist you in finding some answers rather than adding to your questions. As for "self-help," keep in mind that Sigmund Freud analyzed himself. While we do not wish to denigrate all his contributions to psychology (for example, explorations of the unconscious), we suggest that self-analysis contributed weightily to some of the errors that both the anybody-can-do-it believers and those who prefer to work within the system have been fighting for many, many years to correct.

So what about your prospective therapist's credentials? Ask. No one who has suffered the slings and arrows of outrageous preparation for certification is shy about saying. Go to the library and check directories: for example, those published by the American Psychological Association, the Academy of Certified Social Workers, the American Psychiatric Association, as well as local and state directories of various such professions. Is the individual properly licenced or certified? What degree? As a rule of thumb, Ph.D—make sure it's in *clinical* psychology, or that the person underwent post-doctoral clinical training; M.D. (make sure a *psychiatric* residency was completed) or M.S.W. are good guides. However, a degree in theology, an Ed.D., or a Master's degree in an appropriate field should not be overlooked or regarded as "second best," as long as the individual also underwent clinical-internship programs of appropriate duration and under qualified supervision.

Once you are satisfied that your prospective therapist has such credentials and that she or he has personal qualities that make you sense that the the mysterious yet recognizable state called "rapport" can exist between you, how can you be certain that she or he is not a latent sexist? There may be no *sure* test, since some psychotherapists can be just as sneaky (or repressed) as some other people. But we suggest using "Survival Tips for the Conscientious (Non-Sexist) Therapist", as given in *Women Loving Women: A Message to Psychotherapists Distributed at the Annual Convention of the American Psychiatric Association in May 1975*, a booklet published by the National Gay Task Force. Simply ask your prospective therapist how she or he feels about the following:

1. Discard all theories about lesbianism that are based on *patient* samples or on studies of gay men.
2. Consult with lesbians and feminists to design and carry out broad-based representative studies of the lesbian population in general and the lesbian feminist population in particular. (Lesbians have been virtually ignored in studies of homosexuality.)
3. Be supportive of any client who wishes to explore a same-sex relationship. Support any woman's move toward independence.
4. Join the National Gay Task Force in our effort "to oppose the assignment of characteristics and roles on the basis of gender and the discrimination that results from this." Help break down the sex role stereotypes which inhibit free expression for all women and men. . . .
5. Examine any stereotypes you may have about women in general and lesbians in particular.
6. If you are a man, examine yourself for a possible sexual self-interest in discouraging lesbianism. Does lesbianism pose a personal threat to you?
7. Deal honestly with your own homosexual feelings.
8. Actively promote gay civil rights legislation, implementing your organization's positive stand on this issue. . . .
Further inquire, again to quote the booklet: ". . . Would you hesitate to encourage your female client to develop her full human potential, including any kind of educational and career possibilities she had the capability, means and desire for? Would you hesitate to encourage her to explore her feelings of love for other women?"

One final word on therapy: we are painfully aware of the fact that

the farther you live from larger and more "liberal" cities that offer a variety of therapeutic approaches, the harder will be your task to find a suitable therapist. It is our hope, however, that as younger people become increasingly aware of feminism, gay rights and consciousness raising in general, that more and more trainees in clinical psychology and psychiatric residency programs (as well as other disciplines) will subscribe to the ideas outlined by the National Gay Task Force. Therefore we hope that more hospitals, clinics and university settings will house therapists sympathetic to your needs.

Threesomes . . . or more. As a result of contemporary liberation movements, there is an increasing number of lesbians who are deliberately breaking away from monogamous couple patterns and consciously ridding themselves of the emotions monogamy can breed: jealousy, possessiveness, suspicion, dependency, etc. Consciously rejecting the couple system as being too heterosexual in concept, they are actively applying the principles of freed womanhood to their sexual as well as their domestic lives. Certainly a great deal of serious political as well as self-analysis accompanies lesbians' decisions to break with convention and to carry the emotional bonding of sisterhood over into erotic expression. When these women live together, they almost always live collectively and use the group, rather than the couple, as the unit for sharing; they do, however, take pains to avoid monogamous attachment. Another kind of lesbian threesome can happen spontaneously as a result of the erotic overflow an evening of intimacy can stimulate; these situations usually cement friendship further. Threesomes that have their genesis in drunkenness or dope typically greet the dawn with averted eyes and nervous jokes.

Tongues and tonguing If anyone has any doubts about the universality of response to being licked, let her or him listen to a kitten purr as its mother licks it.

The tongue is a muscular organ with muscle bundles extending longitudinally, laterally and vertically; like any muscle, it can tire. At the front it's attached to the floor of the mouth by the frenulum, which you can see and feel (and which, by the way, can be explored in tongue kisses). The frenulum varies in size, as do the width and length of tongues; muscle strength and susceptibility to the gag reflex vary too. All this means that, especially at first before practice makes more perfect, extensive tonguing can leave your throat muscles taut and sore, and your tongue aching.

At the risk of inhibiting some of your ardor, if you want to tongue you should start slowly. In fact, don't start at all until you know your partner is aroused (unless you know from experience that

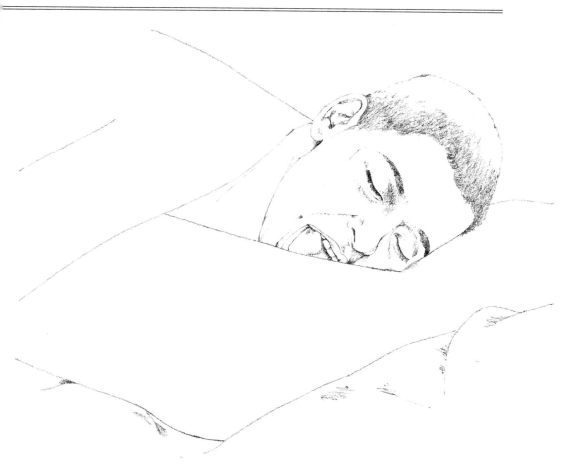

mouth contact arouses her instantly), otherwise you may be at it until it feels like your tongue is going to fall out. Also, start modestly. The very tip of the tongue, along with lip work, works wonders. Be gradual about bringing more of your tongue into play, using more and more as intensity increases, but do not strain the posterior root (the backmost portion of your tongue) with extravagant stretches until the very last moment—if then. Remember, as with that other sex organ, the penis, women contend that it's quality and not quantity that counts. If tongue-fucking is part of the scenario, remember that only the lowest portion of the vagina is sensitive, so you needn't stretch the tongue out too far. Satisfactory tongue work along the vulva and around the clitoris can be achieved without inducing muscle spasms at the back of your tongue.

The key is relaxation. Don't rush. Don't get into a macho act about how much tongue you can give her. And if you can keep a sense of humor about it, stick your tongue out at a mirror: move it round a bit, in and out. See what you can do with comfort and without strain. If you do overdo it, don't worry—the pain will soon pass.

Toys and toy stores   Toys such as vibrators, dildos, edible lotions and other equipment to enhance the enjoyment of sex are readily available in a number of big-city emporia we like to call "toy stores." While a few of them are operated by and for women, most seem to be run on a co-ed basis. We are pleased to report that most male clerks treat women's inspection of, for example, double-headed dildos with no more and no less interest than if they were inspecting bolts of yarn.

Outside big cities, one does not have ready access to toy stores. Solution: order by mail. Most women's newspapers and magazines and various gay publications carry advertising for toy stores; perusing catalogs with your lover can be a turn-on in itself. Lesbians lucky enough to travel abroad will be delighted to discover that toy stores abound in places that used to harbor puritans.

Tribadism   To practice tribadism is to practice rubbing. A tribade is a woman who rubs. Or, in the zipped-up style of the *Shorter Oxford English Dictionary*, a tribade is "a woman who practises unnatural vice with other women."

This is *rubbing*? Wrong-headed, we know; but it is unfortunately typical of standard heterosexual mystification of what lesbians are and what they do, beginning with any attempt to use bodies for pleasure rather than for reproduction. Tribadism today is as out of date in its moral definition as the old *Well of Loneliness* term "invert" or the equally archaic and meaningless "sapphist." But rubbing itself is a sexual reality that begins practically at birth, with babies rocking on their stomachs, feeling the friction of their diaper cloths, and smiling. (Is tribadism really the instance of baby's first smile?) And as we grow we all learn the effects of wrapping our legs around tree trunks and shimmying up or down, or working out on the ropes and exercise bars in the school gym, or riding a horse or a bicycle (especially when your legs are still too short to reach the stirrups or the pedals, and you have to lean forward just a little).

But tribadism is not just a stimulating exercise for growing girls. It can be, and is, called upon as a sophisticated lesbian sexual technique that can even be performed in public. When you cross your legs tightly, you can squeeze your buttocks together a little, swing the leg that's dangling over your knee—and what you are feeling is the consequence of tribadism. Sitting in a bus (the back rows are the best) or in a car on a bumpy highway in a pair of tight jeans, again, cross your thighs tightly. What you are beginning to feel is caused by tribadism; and if it goes on too long what you may have—on that bus, in that car, on that horse, in that lobby or waiting-room—is a mild but definite case of orgasm. Tribadism leading to orgasm is what's meant by "unnatural vice."

A tribade at her most tantalizing is a partner on a dance floor or in a bed; and it is the dance floor that has become the most common scene for tribadic practice among today's lesbians—the slow grind. Effective tribadic dancing consists, naturally, of holding your part-

ner tightly or loosely (more and more tightly as the dance progresses) around the waist; and, from the waist through the pelvic area, gluing and ungluing yourself to her in time to the beat. Simultaneously, your thighs touch, grind, caress, as you rotate between each other's legs at the crotch. Literally, you are wrapped around each other at all possible points, while the hands cleverly assist with pressure and release against the partner's buttocks. Thus is orgasm often choreographed on the most glistening of dance floors. The same effect is achieved when one of you leans against a (very) solid object— a kitchen sink, for instance, or a car—to give both of you support, and you revolve in half-circles on the axis of thigh against clitoris.

Because tribadism—or humping and grinding—is usually enjoyed as a public dodge to get a little (because you can't wait to get home, or because it's impossible to go home together), the pleasure is achieved through clothing. Denim jeans, with their elasticity and their capacity to mold perfectly to your shape (and add a little trip of their own against the clitoris), serve best if you're hoping to make a tribade of yourself. The common heterosexual slang for tribadism is "dry fuck" (because the penis can't erect fully and let loose?), but lesbians know that the experience is anything but dry. Fortunately, the international lesbian uniform will, if necessary, hold your reputation (as well as your private parts) together. Denim camouflages the moisture as easily as it arouses it.

For many lesbians, however, tribadism isn't simply a substitute for sex-in-the-raw or an erotic amulet to protect against boredom on long trips. Many "butch" lesbians, for good reasons of their own, exclusively practice tribadism in bed, achieving orgasm through friction against their "femme's" thigh while making love with their right or left hand and sucking a nipple. Some stay dressed; some don't. Lesbians who wouldn't usually role play—who, indeed, have never considered it—might follow their example and add a variation to their sexual procedure.

Truck driver Or, "diesel dyke." Sometimes derogatory slang, sometimes an affectionate in-joke.

Tucking All the best lovemaking flows from deep feeling for the other person, from affection, from love, from intimacy. Tucking is as much about warmth and sharing as it is about lovemaking. It's a pleasurable game that can be played before or after sex—a kind of demand–response situation a woman can relate to with equal ease, whether tucking or being tucked. And sometimes it's simply a way to make sleeping together a delectable experience, when sex *per se* seems less desirable than being close. Tucking can be as playful as you like (any kind of lovemaking with-

out a liberal dose of playfulness doesn't really qualify) and the basic "best" of this kind of loving goes as follows:

Make up the bed in advance with fresh sheets and pillowcases and, preferably, with a fluffy comforter or quilt plus as many pillows and covers as the climate permits and your tuckee revels in.

The tucker in this situation is the actor entire, providing an excess of luxury and peacefulness for the tuckee, who is the passive recipient. With this in mind you approach your standing partner from the side, slipping an arm around her shoulders, turning her to you so that your breasts kiss. Slowly, in this position, glide to the bed with her, and lower the top sheet and quilt. Giving her as much support as your strength permits, grasp her lightly around the waist and lower her to a sitting position. Then lean and lower her top half against the pillows and, with your free arm, slide her legs under the sheet and quilt.

Now, literally, tuck her in, starting with the feet. Surround her feet with the gentle pressure of the coverings and work your way up, encasing her in comfort as you go. Working slowly, you pause to tuck in some kisses, too. Fold her arms above her abdomen. Make sure the covers are securely tucked beneath her shoulders. Now, all there is to see of your love are her mouth, nose, eyes and the top of her head, all waiting for your kisses.

Lie down beside her, on your side, facing her (*outside* the covers) and survey what you have wrought: she is safely tucked in, you are there—a presence, a protector, if you will, of the tranquillity you have built for her.

Sometimes couples experience tucking as the ultimate in caring tenderness, an act requiring no expansion at all. Other times, those same couples experience it as an unbearably intense turn-on and tear the little nest apart nearly as soon as it's built. Either way (not to mention the variations on this theme the two of you will play) tucking is a game that children may enjoy, but only two loving women can appreciate at its fullest.

Vagina The vagina is not, as it has been assumed, a passive receptacle for the penis. On the contrary, it is (along with its other function as birth canal) an independent sexual organ with its own distinct capacity for expression. Sexually excited, the vagina lubricates itself, changes in color, lengthens, expands; in orgasm, it contracts. But only the vaginal introitus (the entrance) has sensory receptors. Most lesbians feel sexually cheated unless there is some stimulation of the introitus during sexual activity, some delight in the deep sense of fullness a dildo can produce during climax and yet others refuse all penetration. You should ask new partners openly (see also *Fingers*, *Fucking* and *Vibrators*).

Vaginal infections and V.D. Women need to be reassured that *all* women secrete a kind of discharge that is perfectly normal. Although often transparent, it sometimes can be milky-white or slightly yellowish. The secretion increases on sexual arousal; there is nothing imaginary about getting the crotch of your pants soaking wet simply from staring at some appealing Amazon across the dance floor!

But when the normally acidic balance of the vagina is thrown off (by any number of causes, but commonly by generally lowered resistance or some other condition of illness), that moist warm place can become a perfect culture medium for the growth of organisms.

A monilial infection—candidiasis, "thrush"—comes from a yeast-like fungus causing a thick, white, foul-smelling discharge. (Incidentally, this fungus is normally present in the rectum—which is why we've mentioned the old rule about wiping yourself from front to back. For that matter it is usually present in harmless quantities in the vagina itself, but why double the risk?) More "heroic" treatment (to use the medical phrase) includes painting the vulva, vagina and cervix with gentian violet, but orally taken drugs—often combined with the use of vaginal suppositories—are the more common measures. The drug prescribed is usually nystatin. Some women report that acid douches are effective if the infection is caught in time.

Trichomoniasis—caused by a parasitic flagellate protozoa, for those of you with a scientific bent—is usually associated with a vaginal discharge that is foamy or bubbly, or yellowish-green and has an even fouler odor than thrush. Again, the prescribed drug—usually Flagyl—is often taken both orally and by suppository. Unfortunately, "trich" is one of those things you *can* catch by moist towels or wash-cloths; and it frequently leads to persistent urinary tract infection and/or cystitis (an inflammation of the bladder which, again, can be treated fairly simply, but which is both a terrible nuisance and tends to recur). Mild cystitis can sometimes be alleviated by ingesting lots of water, soaking in a tubful of tepid water, and avoiding coffee and tea. Medical attention, which will most likely be confined to antibiotic prescriptions but can be more complicated if the condition is chronic, is advisable.

Lesbians appear to be no less and no more prone to vaginal infections than any other women. They may be somewhat readier to attend to them promptly both because they are generally more in tune with their own bodies (and hence more open to notice when things go wrong) and because they enjoy their sex lives (and hence don't want to put up with anything that might hamper such activity). But just in case, we'll put in a word in favor of quick attention: you owe it not only to yourself but also to your partner. Imagine the dampening effect of sharing a towel that's spreading "trich," or of having a monilial infection erupt in someone's mouth.

As for V.D., especially gonorrhea, which seems to be a scourge of the male gay life-style, lesbians seem to be no more prone than other women; indeed, if anything they are less prone being generally free from the risk of infection by males. Nonetheless it *can* occur, with a lot of pain on urination and from the glandular swelling caused by pus. Antibiotics work miracles, although you should keep in mind that women frequently get vaginitis from ingesting certain antibiotics, though eating yogurt will often offset that effect.

Crabs, or pubic lice, are neither V.D. nor a vaginal infection. Few lesbians have ever even seen one, let alone been infected—probably because women tend to be rather fastidious about personal hygiene. Nonetheless, you *could* catch them—if not from a partner, then from bedding or clothes. This malady does not require medical attention. Effective lotions and creams are readily available at your corner pharmacy.

Simple inflammations—vaginitis or vulvitis—can often be effectively treated by douching and/or applying over-the-counter pharmaceutical products frequently prepared as moistened throw-away "wipes" if not as soothing creams or ointments made specifically for that purpose. Sometimes taking a brief vacation from sexual activity may be necessary if there is redness and swelling of tissue.

Vibrators In the usual literature about sex, vibrators are discussed primarily as legitimate tools for practice, a way by which a woman can learn how to do the real thing. One company that manufactures a vibrator explicitly designed for sex calls it "Prelude." They enclose in the kit a brochure focused on the use of their gadget for curing "frigidity."

All this reflects a restricted view of the pleasures and possibilities of the vibrator—or vibrators, rather, for they come in a multitude of shapes and sizes.

Vibrators are used most often for masturbation (which is rarely just "practice"). The most common type of vibrator is a flesh-colored, plastic, penis-shaped device run by flashlight batteries. This species is readily available in corner drugstores and is usually accompanied by a little sign labeling it a body massager. It is obviously not designed to be a body massager. However, it is also not specifically designed to massage the clitoris and although it can be inserted into the vagina so can any number of similarly shaped objects, not to mention a dildo. Even the fact that it moves is not too much of an advantage, for it won't move optimally for very long periods of time (the batteries tend to run down). It also gets too hot and can sound like a medium-sized lawn mower, which is distracting. But if you

are prepared for the noise factor, such a model can be quite satisfactory—especially if used for relatively brief stretches. It is also quite inexpensive, and women who aren't sure they want to invest much in the vibrator experience might like to start with this type.

A more satisfactory kind of vibrator is the small, compact type with a cord and plug. One version of this looks like a small plastic snub-nosed gun; another version is oval, with a strap through which the guiding hand is slipped. These vibrators are quiet, don't overheat, and can go on forever. They function best on one person at a time, so they're fine for masturbation alone. They can also be used for caressing and stimulating a lover. The smooth rubber heads, which are the primary attachment for the snub-nosed variety, move quickly and finely in a motion that can't be duplicated by a hand but which, when sensitively guided by a hand, is delightful. Vibrators can give pleasure to any part of the body—feet, ribs, crooks of elbows, the small of the back. To prolong the experience a woman should begin with these parts before moving to the area of the genitals, which are quickly aroused by the smooth flutter of the vibrator.

You move the vibrator along the tops of the thighs, over to the insides, and slowly back and forth along the crease where legs meet torso. Then gently along the outer edge of the labia, over the vaginal opening, around the anus, and back up again just to touch the clitoris. This sort of movement will almost always cause a quick arousal, and if a lover is guiding the vibrator and resting on her side beside her partner, her use of the vibrator can be accompanied by caresses and kissing and licking of the lover's face and ears and breasts and navel or whatever seems best to underline her pleasure. Touching the vibrator directly to the clitoris will usually lead to orgasm more quickly than stimulus by hand or mouth. However, direct stimulation can also be startling to women not used to vibrators, and it is wise to use a towel between body and vibrator at first, in order to diffuse the sensation and soften the pressure.

The little snub-nosed vibrator can be used with extra attachments to provide a variety of sensations for a woman alone or for a lover. For instance, a hollow rubber dildo fits over the moving end of the vibrator and can be used for vaginal penetration after the lover is aroused. Initial penetration should be careful and slow, and it sometimes helps to moisten the dildo with saliva or coat it with lubricant. The vibrator causes a steady, quick, whirring movement of the dildo which is simultaneous with the in-and-out movement guided by hand—at first slow and shallow, then deeper and quicker according to what your lover indicates she likes. This can be accompanied by mouth contact with the clitoris—flicks of the tongue in intensity and frequency to coincide with the movement of the vibrator. If alone, more or less the same method can be used if you have two

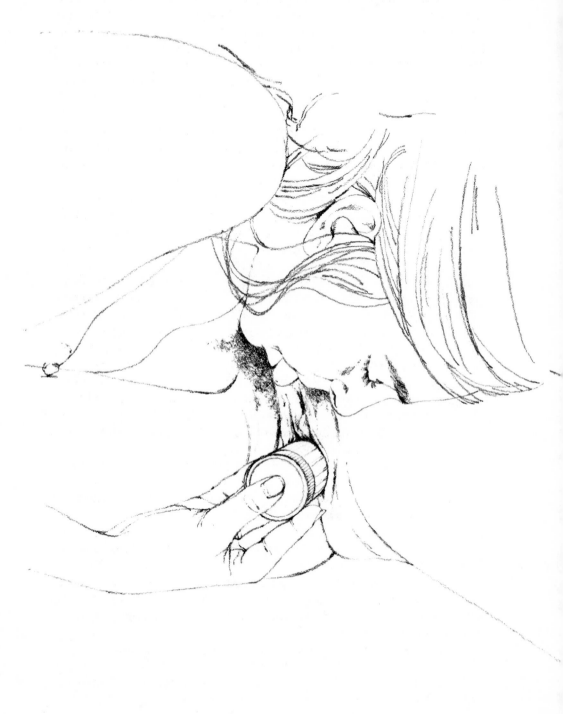

small vibrators—one with the dildo attachment and one with a regular round head to do the work of your absent lover's tongue.

Another kind of vibrator—much bigger, with a long, eighteen-inch handle and a round, yo-yo-like head—can be used by two women simultaneously. If two women lie facing one another, on their sides, or one on top of the other, they can hold the vibrator between them and move their hips so that their genitals are massaged by its head. This model can, of course, be used by a woman alone, but its chief advantage is simultaneous stimulation of both partners.

Multiple orgasms are perhaps more easily reached with a vibrator, since a light vibration can be sustained readily after the initial orgasm and since the little machine doesn't get tired. A word of caution, however. Vibrators can't take the place of a warm, loving body that talks and strokes and kisses and shares breakfast. And the touch of a vibrator is not that of a hand or a tongue. Because it is more intense, one can become dependent on that steady, never-flagging pressure. So use it as a treat, not a staple on the diet.

Voyeurs A voyeur is a peeping Tom. Note the gender: apparently Janes do not slip through darkened alleys to gain access to vantage points suitable for viewing other people undressing in bedrooms.

Nonetheless, divorced from its dirty-old-man connotations, voyeurism simply in the sense of watching something sexy can be a powerful turn-on. If this were not so, lesbians would not enjoy watching other lesbians on a dance floor and you would be indifferent to watching your lover display her nude body. Also we've several times mentioned the stimulating effects of watching your partner masturbate in front of you.

The big difference—even in the case of group sex, for those lesbians who are into it or at least like to experiment—is that in these cases you intend to participate. That's not at all the same as getting your jollies off like a voyeur.

Vulva All of your external genitals are called the vulva by people friendly to it. Those who'd rather you lock it up and throw away the key call the vulva *pudendum*, "a thing of shame." Your vulva (or "covering") consists of the *mons pubis* (or *mons veneris*, mound of Venus), the major and minor lips, the clitoris and the opening to the vagina.

Waking Waking can be delicious or rude. At its delicious best it can be a time for ardent lovemaking (many women claim they feel at their sexiest first thing in the morning), breakfast in bed or any number of other joyful activities. The rude part comes when you, a night person who would just as soon pull the covers over your head to simulate darkness for another three hours of blissful sleep, are roused by blinding light from a thrown sash, a rattling breakfast tray and a disgustingly cheery "Good *mor*ning: time to get *up!*" from your bouncy, morning-person lover.

Time for some serious negotiating. A little compromise can go a long way: you can gradually learn to appreciate some things about the morning just as she can learn to enjoy some things about sleeping-in a little.

For most lesbians, preferred styles of waking are actually a pretty academic matter except on weekends. The alarm goes off and you both dash off to work. We heartily recommend occasionally setting the alarm for a slightly earlier hour so you can both enjoy making love on a weekday morning. Even night persons can discover how much it enhances the waking process.

Water, water, everywhere Judging by sales of whirlpool baths and fancy showerheads one might think that the straight world and/or its entrepreneurs had just discovered the sensual possibilities of water. We sincerely doubt that there is a lesbian alive who has not done it in the bathtub or shower, lake, ocean or swimming pool, if not in all of them. A lesbian archaeologist claims to have enjoyed a particularly stimulating encounter in a desert watering hole, between digs.

Quite apart from the enjoyable sensuality of bathing together, soaping and rinsing each other, two women can assume a variety of positions for sex-to-climax in a bathtub. Facing each other, you can shift to a partial side-to-side position that enables you, legs intertwined, to press against each other, cunt to cunt. Or, squatting face-to-face Indian style, you can use your hands or a double-headed dildo to work on each other. With her face to your back, she can sit on your lap as you reach around her stomach and down to her crotch; you can press against her buttocks for simultaneous stimulation or, if she's agile enough, she can simply slip her arms down around her own back and approach your water-bathed vulva.

If both of you like water and neither one of you is given to little deaths in which you fall over in a swoon, your sexual activities in a shower are almost limitless. You can embrace face-to-face or from behind. You can make love simultaneously, or take turns. Supporting herself against the side of the shower, your lover can arch her back and spread her legs for you to go down on her.

You can lie down and be stimulated nearly (or sometimes all the way) to climax by the shower falling against your clitoris and vulva.

The hand-held shower, directed closer against you, is more effective —and this can easily be set up to do its work as you kneel to suck on your standing partner. But never shoot water directly into a vagina; it's dangerous.

Oceans and salt-water lakes have a particular advantage in that the buoyancy of salt water assists you to assume and maintain any number of positions allowing for sex by hand, by thigh-against-crotch rubbing, by crotch-against-stomach rubbing (she'll be easy to support, legs locked behind you, in the water) or by any other means that strikes your fancy or matches your equipment. We have heard of a number of attempts to go down on a lover underwater, but apparently few women possess the breath-holding capacity to take their lover all the way to orgasm. Besides, some women become so intent on their pleasure and their desire to come that they may grab their lover's head and hold it there until the crucial moment. Drowning your lover is not fair game.

Swimming pools tend to be better equipped than lakes and, given a secure fence to block off curious neighbors, a swimming pool is ideal for outdoor water games. Steps, inner tubes and floating mattresses facilitate activities more difficult to achieve in bigger bodies of water (ocean) or smaller bodies of water (bathtub). For example, one of you sits on the edge of a mattress, legs apart, and the other makes mouth-to-vulva contact, supporting herself by wrapping her arms around you and the mattress. The drawback there is that treading water is tiring and somewhat distracting for women who have trouble concentrating on more than one thing at a time. If you're both agile—and good swimmers, in case of an accidental dunking—lovemaking on a mattress can be almost as much fun as doing it while swimming together, when the stronger swimmer supports the other on her back or stomach.

A lesbian bibliography

A comprehensive listing of all lesbiana is impossible in this context. The most nearly complete bibliography is *The Lesbian In Literature: A Bibliography*, 2nd ed., Damon, Watson, Jordan, eds., P.O. Box 5025, Washington Station, Reno, Nevada 89503, but see also the other bibliographies listed under *Bibliographies and Directories*.

Books

Abbott, Sidney, and Love, Barbara, *Sappho Was A Right-On Woman: A Liberated View of Lesbianism*, Stein and Day, 1972

Anderson, Margaret, *My Thirty Years' War*, Horizon, New York, 1969

Anderson, Margaret, *The Fiery Fountains*, Horizon, New York, 1969

Anderson, Margaret, *The Strange Necessity*, Horizon, New York, 1969

Ansell, Helen, *Lucy*, Harper and Row, 1969

Arnold, June, *The Cook and The Carpenter*, Daughters Inc., 1974

Arnold, June, *Sister Gin*, Daughters Inc., 1975

Barnard, Mary (trans.), *Sappho, A New Translation*, University of California Press, Berkeley, 1958

Barnes, Djuna, *Nightwood*, Harcourt Brace, New York, 1937

Beal, M. F., *Angel Dance*, Daughters Inc., 1977

Birkby, Johnston, Harris et. al., (eds.), *Amazon Expedition: A Lesbian-Feminist Anthology*, Times Change Press, 1973

Brophy, Brigid, *The Snow Ball and The Finishing Touch*, World, New York, 1964

Brown, Rita Mae, *A Plain Brown Rapper*, Diana Press, 1976

Brown, Rita Mae, *In Her Day*, Daughters Inc., 1976

Brown, Rita Mae, *Rubyfruit Jungle*, Daughters Inc., 1974

Bunch, Charlotte, and Myron, Nancy, (eds.), *Lesbianism And The Women's Movement*, Diana Press, 1975

Bunch, Charlotte, and Myron, Nancy, (eds.), *Women Remembered*, Diana Press, 1975

Covina, Gina, and Galana, Laurel, (eds.), *The Lesbian Reader: An Amazon Quarterly Anthology*, Amazon Press, 1975

Crawford, Linda, *In A Class By Herself*, Scribner's, 1976

Foster, Jeannette H., *Sex Variant Women In Literature: A Historical and Quantitative Survey*, Diana Press, 1975

Gay Academic Union, *The Universities and the Gay Experience*, New York, 1974

Gearhart, Sally, and Johnson, William R., (eds.), *Loving Women/Loving Men: Gay Liberation and The Church*, Glide, 1974

Grahn, Judy, *Edward The Dyke*, Women's Press Collective, n.d.

Grahn, Judy, *A Woman Is Talking To Death*, Women's Press Collective, 1974

Grier, Barbara, and Reid, Coletta, (eds.), *Lesbian Lives*, Diana Press, 1976

Grier, Barbara, and Reid, Coletta, (eds.), *The Lavender Herring*, Diana Press, 1976

Grier, Barbara, and Reid, Coletta, (eds.), *The Lesbian's Home Journal*, Diana Press, 1976

Harris, Bertha, *Lover*, Daughters Inc., 1976

Harris, Bertha, *Confessions of Cherubino*, Harcourt Brace, 1972

Harris, Bertha, *Catching Saradove*, Harcourt Brace, 1969

Hite, Shere, *The Hite Report*, Macmillan, 1976

Howard, Elizabeth Jane, *Odd Girl Out*, Viking, 1972

Isabell, Sharon, *Yesterday's Lessons*, Women's Press Collective, Oakland, 1975

Jackson, Shirley, *The Haunting of Hill House*, Popular Library, 1959

Jay, Karla, and Young, Allen, (eds.), *Out of the Closets, Voices of Gay Liberation*, Douglas-Links (Quick Fox), 1972

Jay, Karla, and Young, Allen, (eds.), *After You're Out: Personal Experiences of Gay Men and Lesbian Women*, Douglas-Links (Quick Fox), 1975

Johnston, Jill, *Lesbian Nation: The Feminist Solution*, Simon and Schuster, 1973

Jones, Sonya, *The Legacy*, Vanity Press, Atlanta, 1976

Katz, Jonathan, *Gay American History: Lesbians and Gay Men In The U.S.A.: A Documentary Account*, Crowell, 1976

King, Louise W., *The Velocipede Handicap*, Curtis, New York, n.d.

King, Louise W., *The Day We Were Mostly Butterflies*, Curtis, New York, 1963

Klaich, Dolores, *Woman Plus Woman: Attitudes Toward Lesbianism*, Simon and Schuster, 1974

Larkin, Joan, *Housework*, Out and Out Press, Brooklyn, 1976

Lesbians Speak Out, Women's Press Collective, Oakland, 1974

Linda Marie, *I Must Not Rock*, Daughters Inc., 1977

Martin, Del, and Lyon, Phyllis, *Lesbian/Woman*, Bantam, 1972

Meaker, Marijane, *Shockproof Sidney Skate*, Curtis, 1973

Miller, Isabel, *Patience and Sarah*, Fawcett Crest, 1972

Millett, Kate, *Flying*, Knopf, 1974

Millett, Kate, *Sita*, Farrar, Straus and Giroux, 1977

Nachman, Elana, *Riverfinger Women*, Daughters Inc., 1975

Parker, Pat, *Child of Myself*, Women's Press Collective, Oakland, 1972

Parker, Pat, *Pit Stop*, Women's Press Collective, Oakland, 1973

Pass, Gail, *Zoe's Book*, Houghton Mifflin, 1976

Renault, Mary, *The Middle Mist*, Popular Library, 1972

Rendell, Ruth, *From Doon with Death*, Ballantine, 1965

Rennie, Susan, and Grimstad, Kirsten, *The New Woman's Survival Sourcebook*, Knopf, 1975

Rich, Adrienne, *Of Woman Born, Motherhood as Experience and Institution*, Norton, 1976

Rule, Jane, *Against The Season*, McCall, 1971

Rule, Jane, *Lesbian Images*, Doubleday, 1975

Rule, Jane, *Desert Of The Heart*, World, 1965

Rule, Jane, *This is Not For You*, McCall, 1972

Russ, Joanna, *The Female Man*, Bantam, 1975

Scoppetone, Sandra, *Trying Hard to Hear You*, Bantam, 1976

Shelley, Martha, *Crossing the DMZ*, Women's Press Collective, Oakland, 1974

Sherfey, Mary Jane, M.D., *The Nature and Evolution of Female Sexuality*, Vintage, 1973

Sherman, Susan, *Women Poems Love Poems*, Two & Two Press, 1975

Shockley, Ann, *Loving Her*, Bobbs-Merrill, 1974

Simpson, Ruth, *From the Closet to the Courts: the Lesbian Transition*, Viking, 1975

Solanas, Valerie, *S.C.U.M. Manifesto*, Olympia, 1968

Stein, Gertrude, *Fernhurst, Q.E.D. and Other Early Writings*, Liveright, 1971

Troubridge, Lady Una, *The Life and Death of Radclyffe Hall*, Citadel, N.Y., 1963

Vida, Ginny (ed.), *Our Right to Love: A Lesbian Sourcebook*, Prentice-Hall, N.J., 1977

Vivien, Rene, *A Woman Appeared To Me*, Naiad Press, 1976

Wittig, Monique, *Les Guerillères*, Viking, 1971

Wittig, Monique, *The Lesbian Body*, Peter Owen, London, 1975

Bibliographies and Directories

Bullough, Vern L., et al., *An Annotated Bibliography of Homosexuality*, Garland Publishing, October 1976

Damon, Gene, et al., *The Lesbian In Literature: A Bibliography*, 1975, The Ladder, P.O. Box 5025, Washington Station, Reno, NA. 89503

Gay Airwaves: List Of Regular Gay Broadcasts in U.S., Public Interest Media Project, 3916 Locust Walk, Phila., PA. 19104

Gay And Lesbian-Feminist Organizations List, National Gay Task Force, 80 5th Ave., Rm. 506, New York, N.Y. 10011

Gay Bookstores And Mail Order Services, U.S. And Canada, National Gay Student Center, 2115 S. St., NW Washington D.C. 20008

Gayellow Pages, Box 292, Village Sta., New York, N.Y. 10014

Gay Professional Organizations and Caucuses (U.S.), National Gay
  Task Force, 80 5th Ave., Rm. 506, New York, N.Y. 10011
Gay Rights Protections in U.S. and Canada, National Gay Task
  Force, 80 5th Ave., Rm. 506, New York, N.Y. 10011
Gittings, Barbara, (coordinator), *A Gay Bibliography*, Task Force on
  Gay Liberation, American Library Association, Box 2383, Phila-
  delphia, PA. 19103
Index/Directory to Women's Media, Media Report to Women, 3306
  Ross Place, NW, Washington D.C. 20008
Kunda, Marie J., (ed.), *Women Loving Women: An Annotated Bib-
  liography*, Womanpress, 1975
Student Gay Groups, U.S. and Canada, 1976, National Gay Student
  Center, 2115 S. St., NW, Washington D.C. 20008

Feminist Presses: A Partial Listing
Daughters Inc., 22 Charles St., New York, N.Y. 10014
Diana Press, 4400 Market Street, Oakland, California 94608
Editions Des Femmes, 2, rue de la Roquette, 75011 Paris, France
The Feminist Press, P.O. Box 334, Old Westbury, New York 11568
Frauenoffensive Verlag, Josephsburg Str. 16, 8 München 80, West
  Germany
Iowa City Women's Press, 116½ East Benton, Iowa City, Iowa 55240
Know Inc., P.O. Box 86031, Pittsburgh, Pennsylvania 15221
Women's Press Collective, 5251 Broadway, Oakland, California
  96410

Periodicals
Albatross, (lesbian feminist humor magazine), 82 South Harrison
  St., East Orange, N.J. 07017
ALFA Newsletter, Atlanta Lesbian Feminist Alliance, Box 5502,
  Atlanta, GA. 30307
American Psychiatric Association Gay Caucus Newsletter, R. Pillard
  M.D., 700 Harrison Ave., Boston, MA. 02118
Big Mama Rag, Western Women's News Journal, 1724 Gaylord St.,
  Denver, CO. 80206
The Body Politic, (political analysis and news for gays), Box 7289,
  Sta. A, Toronto, Ont., Canada
The Cellmate, (for women and men in prison), Board of Prison
  Ministry of MCC, Box 36277, Los Angeles, CA. 90036
Christopher Street, (national gay magazine), 60 W. 13th St., New
  York, N.Y. 10011
The Circle: A Lesbian-Feminist Publication, P.O. Box 427, Waterloo
  Quay, Wellington, New Zealand
Come Out Comix, (lesbian comic books), A Woman's Place, 706
  S.E. Grand Ave., Portland, OR. 97214

Country Women, P.O. Box 51, Albion, CA. 95410

Dyke: A Quarterly, ("A magazine of Lesbian Culture and Analysis"), 70 Barrow St., New York, N.Y. 10014

Emergency Librarian, (bibliographic and resource articles for women), 110-14 Chatsworth Drive, Toronto, Ont., Canada

Feminary, (a lesbian-feminist newsletter), Box 954, Chapel Hill, N.C. 27514

Feminist Alliance Against Rape Newsletter, (national focus), P.O. Box 21033, Washington D.C. 20009

FOCUS, (Daughters of Bilitis newsletter), 419 Boylston St., Room 415, Boston, MA. 02116

Gaia's Guide, (up-to-date listings of lesbian organizations, bars, etc. throughout North America, Europe, Australia, Japan), 115 New Montgomery St., San Francisco, CA. 94105

Gay Community News, (gay weekly for the Northeast), 22 Bromfield, Boston, MA. 02108

Gay Health Reports, (newsletter of Gay Public Health Workers), 206 N. 35th, Philadelphia, PA. 19104

Gay News, (major gay newspaper in Europe), 1-A Normand Gardens, Greyhound Rd., London W14 9SB, England

Gays on the Hill, (news of gay civil rights progress in U.S. Congress), Suite 210, 110 Maryland Ave., NE, Washington D.C. 20002

Gay People and Mental Health, (mental health newsletter), Suite 3-B, 490 West End Ave., New York, N.Y. 10024

Gay Tide, (gay liberation newspaper), Box 1463, Sta. A, Vancouver, B.C., Canada

Hecate: A Women's Interdisciplinary Journal, (women's studies), P.O. Box 99, St. Lucia, Queensland, Australia

In Unity, (news and opinion journal of Universal Fellowship of Metropolitan Community Churches), Box 36277, Los Angeles, CA. 90036

It's Time, (newsletter of the National Gay Task Force), 80 5th Ave., Rm. 506, New York, N.Y. 10011

Join Hands, (gay prisoners' news), Box 42242, San Francisco, CA. 94142

Journal of Homosexuality, Haworth Press, 174 5th Ave., New York, N.Y. 10010

Lesbian Connection, (a free monthly newsletter for all lesbians), Ambitious Amazons, Box 811, East Lansing, MI. 48823

The Lesbian Tide, (news and analysis), 8855 Cattaraugus Ave., Los Angeles, CA. 90034

Lesbian Voices, (literary magazine), Box 3122, San Jose, CA. 95116

Long Time Coming, (national Canadian lesbian publication), Box 128, Sta. G, Montreal, Canada

Majority Report, (New York City feminist newspaper), 74 Grove

St., New York, N.Y. 10014

Mom's Apple Pie, (Lesbian Mothers National Defense Fund newsletter), 2446 Lorentz Pl., N. Seattle, WA. 98109

Moonstorm, (reflections on lesbian issues), Box 4201, Tower Grove Station, St. Louis, MO. 63118

Newsletter of the Association of Gay Psychologists, Box 29527, Atlanta, GA. 30359

Off Our Backs, (national feminist newspaper), 1724 20th St., NW, Washington D.C. 20009

Paid My Dues, (women's music journal), Women's Soul Publishing, Inc., P.O. Box 11646, Milwaukee, WI. 53211

Plexus, (Bay area feminist newspaper), 3022 Ashby, Berkeley, CA. 94705

Point Blank Times, lesbian-feminist monthly, Box 14643, Houston, TX. 77021

Prime Time, (for the liberation of women in the prime of life), 168 West 86th St., Apt. 9-A, New York, N.Y. 10024

Quest: A Feminist Quarterly, (feminist political analysis and theory), P.O. Box 8843, Washington D.C. 20003

Sappho, (major lesbian magazine in Europe), BCM/Petrel, London WC1, England

Sexual Law Reporter, (reporting on legal developments in sex-related law), 3701 Wilshire Blvd., Suite 700, Los Angeles, CA. 90010

Signal, (newsletter of Gay Nurses Alliance), Box 17593, San Diego, CA. 92117

Signs: Journal of Women in Culture and Society, (academic quarterly), Univ. of Chicago Press, 5801 Ellis Ave., Chicago, Ill. 60637

Sinister Wisdom, (lesbian journal of politics and art), 3116 Country Club Drive, Charlotte, N.C. 28205

So's Your Old Lady, Lesbian Resource Center, 2104 Stevens Ave., S. Minneapolis, MN. 55404

We Got It!, Lesbian Switchboard, 306 North Brooks St., Madison, WS. 53715

WICCE, (a magazine of sisterly love), Box 15833, Philadelphia, PA. 19103

Womanspirit, (a feminist quarterly on women's spirituality), P.O. Box 263, Wolf Creek, OR. 97497

Women: A Journal Of Liberation, (feminist magazine), 3028 Greenmount Ave., Baltimore, MD. 21218

Women and Film, P.O. Box 4501, Berkeley, CA. 94704

Women in Libraries, (Newsletter of the ALA/SSRT Task Force on Women), Cassell, 150 East 30th St., No. 1-F, New York, N.Y. 10016

Women's Rights Law Reporter, 180 University Ave., Newark, N.J. 07102

Pamphlets

American Civil Liberties Union, *Policy Statement on Homosexuality*, American Civil Liberties Union, April 13, 1975

American Psychiatric Association, *Resolutions On Homosexuality*, American Psychiatric Association, December 15, 1973

Crew, Louie, and Norton, Rictor, (eds.), *The Homosexual Imagination, College English*, November 1974 (special issue)

Fairchild, Betty, *Parents of Gays*, 1975, Parents of Gays, Lambda Rising, 1724 20th, NW, Washington D.C. 20009

Gay Academic Union, *The Universities And The Gay Experience*, Gay Academic Union, 1974

Gay Military Counselor's Manual, Gay Center for Social Services of San Diego, 1976

Gay Parent Support Packet, National Gay Task Force, 80 5th Ave., Rm. 506, New York, N.Y. 10011

Hodges, Beth, (ed.), *Margins Special Focus: Lesbian Writing And Publishing, Margins*, No. 23, August 1975

Hodges, Beth, (ed.), *Sinister Wisdom Special Focus: Lesbian Feminist Writing And Publishing, Sinister Wisdom*, Vol. 1, No. 2, November 1976

Martin, Del, and Lyon, Phyllis, *Lesbian Love and Liberation*, Multi Media Resource Center, 1973

Motive: Lesbian Feminist Issue, Motive Inc., 1972

National Council of Churches, *A Resolution on Civil Rights Without Discrimination As To Affectional or Sexual Preference*, National Council of Churches of Christ, U.S.A., March 6, 1975

National Gay Task Force, *Corporate Business Support Statements Packet*, 80 5th Ave., Rm. 506, New York, N.Y. 10011

Theological-Pastoral Resources, Dignity National, 755 Boylston, Boston, MA. 02116

United States Civil Service Commission, *Press Release On New Guidelines For Federal Employment*, U.S. Civil Service Commission, July 3, 1975

Working Paper On Homosexuality, Pacific Yearly Meeting (Friends) Ministry and Oversight Committee, 1975

The Arno Special Collection, 1811-1975

Katz, Jonathan, (ed.), *Homosexuality: Lesbians And Gay Men In Society, History and Literature*, Arno Press, 1975

The 54 books and two periodicals in this series may be purchased individually or as a collection. For a fully annotated brochure with prices and ordering information, write to: Arno Press, 330 Madison, New York, N.Y. 10017. Below are some of the titles:

Acosta, Mercedes de, *Here Lies The Heart*, 1960

Bannon, Ann, *I Am A Woman*, 1959

Bannon, Ann, *Journey To A Woman*, 1960

Bannon, Ann, *Odd Girl Out*, 1957

Bannon, Ann, *Women In The Shadows*, 1959

Barney, Natalie Clifford, *Aventures de l'Esprit*, 1929

Barney, Natalie Clifford, *Traits et Portraits*, 1963

Brooks, Romaine, *Portraits, Tableaux, Dessins*, 1952

Casal, Mary, *The Stone Wall*, 1930

Craigin, Elisabeth, *Either Is Love*, 1937

Daughters of Bilitis, *The Ladder*, vols. 1-16, including an *Index To The Ladder* by Gene Damon, 1956-1972 (nine vols.)

Documents of the Homosexual Rights Movement in Germany, 1836-1927, 1975

Ellis, Havelock, and Symonds, John Addington, *Sexual Inversion*, 1897

Frederics, Diana, *Diana: A Strange Autobiography*, 1939

A Gay Bibliography: Eight Bibliographies on Lesbianism and Male Homosexuality (reprints), 1975

A Gay News Chronology, 1969-1975, index and abstracts of articles from *The New York Times*, 1975

Gordon, Mary, *Chase Of The Wild Goose*, 1936

Government Versus Homosexuals, an original Arno Press anthology, 1975

Gunn, Peter, *Vernon Lee: Violet Paget, 1856-1935*, 1964

A Homosexual Emancipation Miscellany, c. 1835-1952, an original Arno Press anthology, 1975

Katz, Jonathan, *Coming Out!*, 1975

Lesbianism and Feminism In Germany, 1895-1910, an original Arno Press anthology, 1975

Mallett, Françoise, *The Illusionist*, 1952

Mattachine Society, *Mattachine Review*, vols. 1-13, 1955-1966, published as six vols.

Mayne, Xavier, *The Intersexes*, 1908

Morgan, Claire, *The Price Of Salt*, 1952

Olivia, *Olivia*, 1949

Sagarin, Edward, *Structure and Ideology in an Association of Deviants*, 1975

Sturgeon, Mary C., *Michael Field*, 1921

Sweet, Roxanna Thayer, *Political and Social Action in Homophile Organizations*, 1975

Tobin, Kay, and Wicker, Randy, *The Gay Crusaders*, 1972

(Vincenzo), Una, Lady Troubridge, *The Life Of Radclyffe Hall*, 1963

Vivien, Renée, *Poèmes De Renée Vivien*, two vols. in one, 1923-1924

Weirauch, Anna Elisabet, *The Outcast*, 1933

Weirauch, Anna Elisabet, *The Scorpion*, 1932

Wilhelm, Gale, *Torchlight to Valhalla*, 1938
Wilhelm, Gale, *We Too Are Drifting*, 1935
Winsloe, Christa, *The Child Manuela*, 1933

Articles

Basile, R. A., "Lesbian Mothers I," and "Lesbian Mothers II," *Women's Rights Law Reporter*, Vol. 2, No. 2 (December 1974), and Vol. 3, No. 1 (September 1975)

Connexion, May 1973: "The Lesbian and God the Father," "Gay, Proud and Christian," "No Smog in Irvine," "God's Gays"

"The Constitutionality of Laws Forbidding Private Homosexual Conduct," *Michigan Law Review* 72: 1613-1637, August 1974

Guttag, Bianca, "Homophobia in Library School," in: *Revolting Librarians*, Celeste West and Elizabeth Katz, (eds.), Booklegger Press, 1972

Hunter, Nan, and Polikoff, Nancy, "Custody Rights of Lesbian Mothers: Legal Theory and Litigation Strategy," *Buffalo Law Review*, Vol. 25, No. 3, Spring 1976

Klaich, Dolores, "Parents Who Are Gay," *New Times*, July 23, 1976, 34-42

Lawrence, John C., "Homosexuals, Hospitalization and the Nurse," *Nursing Forum*, Summer 1975, 305-317

"The Legality of Homosexual Marrriage," *Yale Law Journal* 82, 573-589, 1973

LeShan, Eda J., "Homosexuality," in her: *Natural Parenthood: Raising Your Child Without A Script*, Signet, 1970

Lester, Elenore, "Gays in the Synagogue," *Present Tense: The Magazine of World Jewish Affairs*, Autumn 1974

Lyon, Phyllis, and Martin, Del, "The Realities of Lesbianism," in: *The New Women: A Motive Anthology Of Women's Liberation*, Charlotte Bunch and Joanne Cooke, (eds.), Bobbs-Merrill, 1970

Ramsey, Judith (as told to), "My Daughter Is Different," *Family Circle*, November 1974

Rashke, Richard, "Homosexuality and the Church of Today," *National Catholic Reporter*, March 26, April 2, 9 and 23, 1976

Secor, Cynthia, "Lesbians: The Doors Open," *Change*, February 1975, 13-17

"Security Clearances for Homosexuals," *Stanford Law Review*, 25: 403-429, February 1973

We'll Do It Ourselves: Combating Sexism in Education, includes: "The Oppression of Gay People," "Literature and Our Gay Minority," "The Gay Student Group," "Afterthought: Lesbians as Gays and as Women," "The Acanfora Case," published by Student Committee, Study Commission on Undergraduate Education and the Education of Teachers, 1974

Index

Abstinence, 41
Aging, 88
Alcohol, 17, 68
Anus, 18, 101, 173
Aphrodisiacs, 20
Après-midi d'une lesbienne, 20-1
Armpits, 21, 32; *see also* Deodorants
Arousal, 23, 32, 63, 100, 152, 162, 173

Backs, back rubs, 23-5; *see also*
   Massage
Bars, 25-7, 54
Bathrooms, sex in, 176-8
Beds, 28-9, 167-8
Big toe, 29-31, 136
Bisexuality, 28, 31-2, 51
Biting, 32
Blowing, 32-3
Bondage, 33-5, 148
Boots, 35
Breakfast in bed, 35-6; *see also* Waking
Breast, 36-7, 61, 92, 127 (mastectomy)
Bunch, Charlotte, 15
Bush, 32, 38-9, 89
Butch, 35, 40, 47-8; *see also* Femme,
   Kiki, Roles
Buttocks, 41, 92, 164, 176

Celibacy, 41
Cheeks, 41
Children of lesbians, 43-5; *see also*
   Legal matters *and* Lesbian
   motherhood
Civil rights, 45
Cleanliness, 47
Clit lit, 47-8
Clitoris, 48-50, 81-4, 95, 176; *see also*
   Frigidity, Masturbation, Sucking
Closets, 50-1
Clothes, 51, 132, 145, 166; *see also*
   Boots, Leather, Nudity
Coming out, 50, 52-7, 122, 134
Consciousness raising, 57-9
Crème de la crème, 60; *see also*
   Demitasse
Crushes, 61, 145
Cunt, 61, 154, 176

Dancing, 27, 61-3, 132, 150, 165

Deodorants, 21-2, 63-4
Depression, 94
Dildos, 84, 117, 130, 136, 157; *see also*
   Toys and toy stores
Discipline, 64, 148
Discrimination, 45, 102-3
Display, 64-5
Drag, 65-6; *see also* Roles
Dressed sex, 66; *see also* Tribadism
Drugs, 66-8
Dykes, 45, 68

Ears, 68
Erogenous zones, 36, 88, 152
Eroticism, 61, 86, 97, 152
Eyes, 61, 69, 89, 92, 150

Fantasy, 70-1
   and Bondage, 34
   and Flagellation, 75-6
   and Little theater, 113
   and Sadomasochism, 148
Feathers, 32, 64, 100, 136
Feminism and lesbianism, 71-2
Femme, 40
Fidelity, 72, 119
Fingers, 72-5, 83, 89, 95, 117; *see*
   also Hands
Finishing off, 75, 157
Flagellation, 75-6
Foreplay, 76-7
Frequency of sex, 77-80
Freud, Sigmund, 12, 80-1, 159
Friendship, 80, 91
Frigidity, 80-1
Fucking, 81-6

Genitalia, 17, 47
Gentleness, 76-88
Growing older, 88-9

Hair:
   head, 89-90
   pubic, 32, 38-9
Hall, Radclyffe, 47, 51, 53, 113, 143, 164
Handicapped lesbians, 91
Hands, 83, 89, 95, 146; *see also*
   Fingers *and* Massage

Heterosexuality:
  Coming out, 52-6
  Consciousness raising, 57
  Sexism, 150
Holding out, 91-2
Horniness, 92
Hugging, 92; *see also* Tribadism
Hygiene, 47
Hysterectomy, 94

Ice cubes, 77
Intimacy, 27, 95, 157, 166

Jealousy, 110, 123
Joy of Sex, The, 21, 50, 140

Kiki, 40
Kissing, 89, 95-100, 148, 168

La plume de ma tante, 100-1, 109; *see also* Feathers
Leather, 102
Legal matters, 102-3
Legs and thighs, 104-6
Lesbian motherhood, 45, 106-12; *see also* Children of lesbians *and* Legal matters
Lesbian myths, 134-5
Lesbos, 112
Little death, 112, 154, 176
Little theater, 113-4; *see also* Seduction
Loneliness, 26, 48, 119
Lotions, 26, 126, 164
Love, 28, 115, 134, 148, 166
Lovemaking:
  as opposed to "having sex," 28, 31, 88, 129, 139
  Foreplay, 76
  Waking, 175
  see also Romance
Lubrication, 88, 117-8

Making love, *see* Lovemaking
Marriage, 118-22; *see also* Fidelity
Married lesbians, 122-3
Masochism, *see* Sadomasochism
Massage, 123-6; *see also* Backs
Mastectomy, 127
Masturbation, 128-30
  alone, 77, 80, 88
  before lover, 30, 86, 148;

  see also Celibacy *and* Vibrators
Menopause, 88, 130
Menstruation, 130-1
Mirrors, 131-2
Mound of Venus, 132
Mouth, 36, 173
  Biting, 32
  Kissing, 95-7
  Sucking, 154
Multiple orgasms, 132, 175
Myths about lesbianism, 134-5

Navel, 135-6
Nose, 137
Nudity, 137

Oophorectomy, 94
Orgasm, 112, 137-9
  Clitoral, 80-1, 86, 106
  Multiple, 132, 175
  "Vaginal," 80-1
Out in the open, 139

Perfumes, 139-40
Physical handicaps, 91
Pillow talk, 140-1
Play, 142-3
Pornography, 143-4; *see also* Clit lit *and* Fantasy
Promiscuity, 144
Puberty, 144-5
Pubic hair, 32, 38-9, 89

Quickies, 66, 145-6

Role-playing, 65, 91, 146, 166; *see also* Sharing
Roles, 146-8
Romance, 148; *see also* Love
Rousseau, Jean-Jacques, 12

Sadomasochism, 32, 91, 148
Sappho, 56, 112, 150
Seduction, 149-50
Sexism, 150
Sexual anatomy, 17
Sharing, 27, 146
Shaving, 21, 106
Sitting pretty, 151
Sixty-nining, 154

Skin, 32, 140, 152-3
Smells, 21-2; *see also* Perfumes
Sprenger, Jacob, 10, 11, 14
Standing-up sex, 154
Stereotyping, 63, 160
Straight women, 92, 134, 144
Sucking, 28, 97, 100, 137, 154-7

Tenderness, 77; *see also* Gentleness
Therapy, 158-62
Tomboys, 53
Tongues and tonguing, 162-3
Toys and toy stores, 164
Trade-off, 35, 36, 148; *see also* Sharing
Tribadism, 37, 164-6
Truck driver, 166
Tucking, 166

Uterus, 94, 131

Vagina, 168; *see also* Genitalia
Vaginal infections and V.D., 170-1
Vibrators, 86, 136, 151, 154, 171-5; *see also* Toys and toy stores
Voyeurs, 175
Vulva, 76, 135, 157, 163, 175

Waking, 175-6
Well of Loneliness, The, 47, 53, 113, 143, 164
Wetness, 83, 117, 131